# Competitive Branding

# Competitive Branding

Winning in the market place
with value-added brands

Torsten H. Nilson
Nilson Consulting Ltd, Surrey

JOHN WILEY & SONS
Chichester • New York • Weinheim • Brisbane • Singapore • Toronto

*Other Wiley Editorial Offices*

John Wiley & Sons, Inc., 605 Third Avenue,
New York, NY 10158-0012, USA

Weinheim • Brisbane • Singapore • Toronto

**British Library Cataloguing in Publication Data**
A catalogue record for this book is available from the British Library

ISBN  0-471-984574

Typeset in Linotype Palatino 11/13pt by Stephen Wright-Bouvier of the
Rainwater Consultancy, Faringdon, Oxfordshire.
Printed and bound in Great Britain by Biddles Ltd, Guildford and King's Lynn.
This book is printed on acid-free paper responsibly manufactured from sustainable
forestry, for which at least two trees are planted for each one used.

# Contents

Preface                                                           vii

Acknowledgements                                                  xi

Part 1   The basics – Value-added Marketing                        1
         Introduction                                              3
   1.    Competitive branding and cost-effective marketing         5
   2.    The three phases of marketing                            13
   3.    The importance of being Number 1                         19
   4.    Brand management – creating preference                   25
   5.    Value-added marketing                                    31
   6.    Understand!                                              35
         Summary                                                 41

Part 2   Competitive brand development                           43
         Introduction                                            45
   1.    Why branding?                                            47
   2.    The origins of branding – a (very) brief history         57
   3.    Building brands                                          63
   4.    The brand values                                        73
   5.    Pricing in the brand development process                 83
   6.    Brand terminology                                        87
   7.    The brand hierarchy                                      99
   8.    Brand stretching                                        103
   9.    International brand strategies                          109
  10.    Managing the brand development process                  115
         Summary                                                 121

Part 3   Making the brand competitive                    123
          Introduction                                   125
   1.     Getting the foundation right                    127
   2.     The marketing mix                               139
   3      Product development – an introduction           147
   4.     New product development (NPD)                   153
   5.     Old product development (OPD)                   159
   6.     Communication – an introduction                 165
   7.     Personal selling                                169
   8.     Sales promotion                                 173
   9.     Advertising                                     181
  10.     PR – public relations                           189
  11.     Word-of-mouth                                   193
  12.     Direct marketing                                199
  13.     Design                                          205
  14.     Distribution                                    209
  15.     Generating revenues                             213
  16.     Managing the brand                              221
          Summary                                         225

Conclusions                                              227

Reading suggestions                                      229

Index                                                    231

# Preface

Competitiveness is the key to business success and strong brands can make the difference between winning and losing in the market place. Like most good and useful ideas, the basic concept of branding is a simple one. The brand is the symbol of a company or product(s) and a tool to build and communicate the trust and the reputation of the items and/or services. The challenge is to avoid complicating the branding process too much and to ensure that the creation and implementation – making the brands competitive – is done with the right mix of creative flair and systematic marketing. Hopefully the book will help you to achieve this.

My objective with the book is to provide useable, practical and well-founded advice and methods for building brands that will succeed in the increasingly competitive market place. The concepts and models in the book are the result of observing successful brands, analysing what has made them successful and then transforming that knowledge into practical advice, applicable to all the difficult situations today's brand management is facing. I have also included numerous examples to illustrate the various points, some of them have had to be disguised but they are all actual examples unless specifically defined as fictitious.

Most of the examples in the book refer to consumer goods. The reason is that consumer goods, in the main, are better known and data are more generally available. This does not mean that this book is for consumer goods branding only. Far from it. We have also successfully implemented competitive brand strategies in the business-to-business sector, following the principles described in the book.

The book is in three parts. The first part is a short resumé of some of the main aspects of successful marketing, the second provides a framework for competitive branding and in the third part I have elaborated on how to build successful brands by using the marketing mix effectively. In addition at the end of each part I have given a very brief summary and there is at the end of the book a list of books that you might find interesting and/or useful. It is not a formal bibliography, just a list of suggestions.

*Competitive Branding* shares some basic principles with my previous books, in particular *Value-added Marketing*. However, since writing *Value-added Marketing*, I have developed the 'value-added' concept further and, in particular, linked it to building strong, competitive brands. In the process I have gained new insights and also collected many new examples which I trust will prove beneficial and useful.

In this book I make a distinct difference between brand management and brand managers. Brand management is a key responsibility in any company and can involve CEOs, marketing directors and any other executive with significant responsibility for one or several brands. Brand managers, on the other hand, are usually fairly junior executives in a marketing department, sometimes with influence and sometimes not. I do hope that brand management as well as brand managers will find the book of use but please note the distinction.

One other semantic issue is that I have used the term 'product' in a very generic sense. On occasion, where particularly appropriate, I have added and/or service but please note that 'product' is not exclusively traditional products but is used generically for products, services, product/service packages and any other concept a company might sell, including 'solutions' which is increasingly the real 'product', especially in business-to-business marketing.

I would also like to add that if I have been overzealous in explaining marketing expressions and the background to brands, please accept my apologies. If terminology and brand expressions have been left unexplained, I have done so to avoid boring those familiar with the jargon and the market place.

I have enjoyed writing this book and I sincerely hope it will help You and Your Company to win the marketing battle.

Torsten H. Nilson
Oxted, Surrey
July 1998

# Acknowledgements

I would like to thank all those who have make this book possible. I am extremely grateful to all my colleagues and clients, who over the years – knowingly and unknowingly – have contributed with information, views and ideas.

The examples in the book come from a variety of sources. Some come from my own consultancy and line management experience while others are based on what friends and colleagues have told me. Many have their origins in newspapers, magazines and books. In particular I would like to mention *The Economist, Financial Times, Harvard Business Review, Wall Street Journal*, the Swedish *Veckans Affärer*, the UK trade journals *Marketing, Marketing Week, Campaign, Marketing Business, The Grocer* and *Checkout* as well as the IPA Advertising Works book series. I have also found Interbrand's 'The world's greatest brands' an interesting and useful source of brand information.

For insight into and information on relationship marketing I wish to thank Nigel Gatehouse at DunnHumby Associates in London. I would also like to thank Claire Plimmer and her colleagues at John Wiley for their cheerful support.

Management theory states that one activity has to be at the expense of another. Consequently a big thank you to my family, Annika, Towe, Bobo, Finn and Tord.

# Part 1
## The basics –
## Value-added Marketing

# INTRODUCTION

Starting to develop a competitive brand can be a waste of time and resources if it is not based on a sound and business-orientated marketing approach. That is why the first part of this book is about the basics, the marketing approach.

The value-added concept is at the core of successful marketing. As explained in my book *Value-added Marketing* (1992) the classical definition of marketing – fulfilling the needs and wants of customers at a profit – is not enough in today's competitive world. What the successful company must do is to constantly ensure that it is adding tangible and abstract values to the products and service it supplies, and in doing so ensuring that it is offering customers superior perceived value.

This part of the book will outline the key aspects of value-added marketing and how it relates to competitive branding.

# 1
## Competitive branding and cost-effective marketing

Branding is one of the most used words in the marketing executives' vocabulary and, in my experience, cost-effectiveness is one of the least used; however, the two go together. Strong brands are cost-effective marketing tools, as I will demonstrate later, and to build strong brands you need to work cost-effectively as otherwise the strong brand will be owned by a financially weak company which will not be able to sustain the investments in brand building.

## THE BRAND

In recent years, 'brands' have taken on almost mythical proportions. Ever since the late 1980s when companies started to pay well over the asset value for companies with strong brands, the concept of brands and what they actually are have generated much interest.

A brand is really just a symbol, but a symbol with tremendous potential. This symbol can be expressed in many different ways, it can represent many different value dimensions and it can be something the company nurtures and builds or exploits and neglects. However, regardless of what is built into the brand, it remains in essence a symbol for a company (such as British Airways), a product range (BMW 5-series), a singular product (the Mars bar), an individual (Michael Jackson – the artist), a group of people (McKinsey – the consultants), a set of services

(Hertz car rentals), or a combination of all these and perhaps others as well.

Discussing and reading about branding one easily gets the impression that branding is something that is the sole preserve of: (a) fast moving consumer goods (FMCG), and (b) marketing departments. While branding as an activity first became 'professionalized' in the FMCG area due to foresighted men such as Messrs Procter & Gamble and Lord Leverhulme, as an activity it covers all types of businesses – and always has. Branding is as important for the local builder trying to establish his reputation as it is for multinational high-tech companies such as Microsoft.

A good brand represents trust. Trust is an essential part of successful branding, not only from the perspective of the suppliers but also from the customers. A detailed study on supply chain management in the car industry reported in *Harvard Business Review* concluded that a high level of trust can bring important benefits. 'Relationships with higher levels of trust had substantially lower costs', 'Trust . . . adds value to the relationship' and 'Trust . . . brought potentially important benefits to both sides'.

As will become apparent from this book, branding is not just a marketing activity. It is something that relates to the whole company as, hopefully, all activities within the company have some impact on the product and/or service that is provided. Every little part of the company is part of the branding process and has some impact – if not, the activity should stop immediately as it would represent a waste of time and money.

We see brands all around us, not only in the supermarket as consumers and in our businesses, but in all aspects of everyday life. The rise of the professional marketing machine to support politicians is a well-established phenomenon in most countries but for instance artistes from Rembrandt and Mozart to Elvis Presley, Madonna and Picasso also have all established themselves with the help of a branding process. This process – the brand development – in business terms represents all the activities of the company, or part of a company, to build the reputation and the values the brand symbolizes.

## BRANDING – GETTING MORE AND MORE IMPORTANT

While branding as a set of activities has been around for a very long time, increasing attention has been given to the process in recent years. There are several reasons for this, the main ones being as follows:

- A tremendous amount of commercial messages. It is reported that the average US citizen is exposed to 3,000 commercial messages per day. The figure might well be lower in other parts of the world but we can safely assume that in most countries with a 'commercial infrastructure' the average person will have at least 1,000–2,000 commercial messages beamed at him/her every day. One hundred years ago it might have taken a year to get to the same level and only on the local market day would the people have got close to the cascade of messages we experience every day.

- Product and brand proliferation. Twenty years ago the average supermarket in Europe carried 3-5,000 items, today an average UK supermarket carries some 20-25,000 items. In other words, the average consumer is exposed on his/her shopping trip to four to eight times as many offerings as twenty years ago and needs ways to cope with identifying all the different items on offer.

- Decreasing product differentiation. Although the trend towards product nivellation is much slower than most experts predict and there are still many ways of making one product or service better than another, the fact remains that the difference between the 'poor' and the 'good' alternative in most market sectors has narrowed significantly. 'The bad products are not as bad as they used to be.' For instance in the car industry brands such as the Czech Skoda, that used to be considered bottom of the pile, get reviews from motor journalists that show that the car is a solid and relevant alternative. Of course a Skoda is not a BMW but the difference is less than 30 years ago. This aspect has two implications. The first one is that as the differences are smaller and less noticeable you have to work harder to differentiate your superior product, and to do this you need a brand. The second is that as the tangible aspects of the product or service are becoming more similar, the intangible aspects, the abstract values, are increasing in importance. For instance, in the jeans market Levi's has over the last ten years consistently – especially outside the US – built strong abstract values into the Levi's brand to ensure a distinct profile to justify a premium price.

- The economies of scale has moved away from manufacturing to communication, selling and distribution. The aspect of economies of scale will be developed further later in this book but here it is sufficient to note that as manufacturing technology is becoming increasingly flexible and in many cases with a lower capital base, the costs for marketing and distributing a product is increasing, pushing the need to utilize the economies of scale in this part of the business mix. In short, and very simplistically, to create a brand for a small product costs as much as it does for a big one.

All of these aspects are well-known and recognized. They have a direct impact on the industry but also indirectly they affect everybody. All individuals are consumers and as such exposed to the barrage of commercial messages, so even if you are 'just' a local supplier of business services, your business will be affected. Not everybody realizes that with such a development in the society, every company wishing to survive in the medium term must consider how best to build the brand that is to symbolize the activities of the company in the future. Building a Brand is a concern for every business.

## THE ROLE OF THE BRAND

A brand is a necessity for a business and – whether the manager likes it or not – a business will have a brand profile. Working actively with the brand, rather than in the classical business sense leaving it to the customers to work out what to think about the company, will give the organization some distinct advantages.

The advantages can be summarized in two categories, first it is financially beneficial for the company, and second it gives the employees a sense of purpose. While the former aspect is well-recognized it is worth considering what a well-defined brand can do to a company. A brand that the employees can be proud of, and feel a sense of belonging to, can have considerable positive effect on the morale in a company. We see this especially in entrepreneurial types of organizations. One example is the Virgin group where founder Richard Branson's very high profile and clear statements about company purpose serve as a morale booster for the whole group. Similar effects appear to be at play at Microsoft, where a strong sense of identity with the company – and consequently with the brand – pushes employees to high levels of productivity and, not least, loyalty.

The financial benefits of a strong brand has been covered in other books and in several articles so only a few aspects are mentioned. A strong brand in a market sector creates barriers to entry. The stronger the brand values of the leading brands in a sector – in other words, the stronger the reputation of and trust in the main competitors – the more difficult it is for other players to enter the market.

Brands also often represent continuity which is important in the sense of keeping customer relations; brands are often much older than the company handling them. The average age of a brand is, of course, different from market sector to market sector, but as an example the average age of the top twenty grocery brands in the UK is around sixty years, significantly longer than the reported average age of twenty years for a company listed on the stock market.

Finally, in this respect it is worth repeating the effects of economies of scale. Having a strong brand does create economies of scale, not least in communication. A well-established and correctly built brand will in an instant communicate a distinct set of values (such as trustworthy, reliable and leading-edge) much quicker and more effectively than any expensive commercial. From this, and all other aspects covered in this book, it is hopefully apparent to everyone that the brand is a strategic business tool and to develop a brand is a strategic business activity. It is not the prerogative of the marketing department; as it is fundamental to the business success it must be the concern of top management.

## COST-EFFECTIVENESS

Over time marketing departments have in many organizations acquired a reputation for not being concerned about costs in general and cost-effectiveness in particular. The reasons are many, from pure ignorance as to the need for what is seen as expensive advertising campaigns to real concern due to the difficulties in knowing what is truly cost-effective marketing and brand building.

However, even if the cost-effectiveness sometimes can be difficult to measure that is not a reason for not constantly striving for a more effective use of marketing resources, both when it comes to allocating resources to various activities and then the deployment of the resources to achieve a specific objective. The theme of cost-effectiveness will appear throughout the book. It is a philosophy more than a technique. It is of course essential in order to build a brand profitably and it is also a help in defining objectives. You cannot be cost-effective unless you measure the results of your activities and keep internal and external suppliers 'on their toes'.

### The relevance of brand building to the business-to-business sector

Although traditionally the technique to build brands has been based on fast moving consumer goods (FMCG) a number of factors has made it even more relevant to other business sectors in recent years.

The tremendous impact of the information over-flow society has already been referred to but there are other reasons as well.

The main one is that in a professional buying environment the element of 'buying the right thing/service' is much more important than in a private situation. If a housewife buys a pack of fish fingers and the family at home are not happy with dinner that evening, this is hardly a catastrophe. The risk for the housewife in choosing an unknown brand is limited.

The same situation in a professional situation can be very different. Take the example of a purchasing manager buying office paper for his/her company. On delivery it turns out that the paper jams the photocopiers and the reports the company is producing come out in poor quality print. Inevitably there will be complaints from other departments. If in such a situation it turns out that the buyer has been buying from an unknown paper-mill with limited trading history, his/her boss will be very critical of the buying decision. On the other hand, if the product has come from a reputable supplier, one that has been supplying the company or other well-known companies in the past, the reputation of the buyer will most probably not suffer, it will all be put down to unfortunate circumstances. The branding effect has taken place!

A professional buyer operates in an environment where it is important to be seen to make the right decisions, to buy products and services which to his/her peers, bosses and subordinates make sense. A strong brand will provide a reassurance that can have an enormous impact when a buyer has to choose between two objectively fairly similar offers.

During the 1970s the saying was that 'no one ever got fired for buying an IBM computer'. Due to the problems of IBM in later years the saying does not hold true any more. At the moment it is more likely that no one will get fired for buying Microsoft software or computers with Intel processors but the principle behind the saying is still true. If a brand has a very strong market position, the professional buyer is likely to choose that brand in preference to less known and 'reputable' suppliers.

The conclusion is obvious. Successful companies, regardless of operating in the consumer or the business-to-business market sector, have always nurtured and built their brand profile and will increasingly do so. In the business-to-business sector this has in the main, so far, been done in an intuitive and *ad hoc* way, while among the larger consumer goods companies we have seen more of a systematic approach. This is changing rapidly and an increasing number of business-to-business suppliers are adapting a more aggressive and well-defined approach, making brand development a strategic issue for all businesses.

# 2
# The three phases of marketing

During the twentieth century we have seen marketing developing as an activity from a strictly functional discipline to one encompassing the whole company. In respect of the focus of the activities we have also seen a change, schematically split in three different phases (see Figure 2.1).

| Phase | Activity | Focus |
|---|---|---|
| First | Sell | Company |
| Second | Adapt | Customer |
| Third | Improve | Competition |

**Figure 2.1** *Phases of marketing activity*

Each of the three phases has contributed to the development of the marketing discipline and to appreciate where we are today and what is required of marketing executives a more detailed understanding of the three phases can be helpful.

The first phase, in leading companies covering the period up to around 1960, the role of marketing was to support the sales function in getting the output of the factory or the service centre sold. The style was functional with marketing keeping to its then assignment of inventing ways of making the company's products as attractive as possible. With the benefit of hindsight this might seem an easy task as it was well-defined and there was a distinct focus to the activities. Perhaps it was this focus and clarity which meant that the practitioners, also with the benefit of hindsight, developed great skills in communication and promotion. Virtually all promotional techniques we use today were invented during this period and we also saw a number of great advertising campaigns being created. If you want to improve your crafts-manship in the creation of sales promotion and advertising, a close study of this period can bring up some interesting ideas which can be transformed into today's market place.

While many companies went away from this model in the 1960s, and later, there are still many companies following this way of working. Integrated marketing involving all parts of the company is still not universally accepted and many companies only pay lip-service to taking customer views into account when it comes to defining the product or service output.

The second phase is known as 'classical marketing'. It is repre-sented by the methods and theories taught at marketing courses around the globe. The best exponent is Professor Philip Kotler's standard text book *Marketing Management*. The approach of focusing on fulfilling customer needs and wants was seen as quite revolutionary at that time as up until then the only worry for the marketers was to sell what the company produced. Now, the idea was to look at the total process so that only products fulfilling a need and really wanted by the customers would be produced, and if so, the customers would be happy to buy and pay. The latter being increasingly important as not only did the theory say that you had to fulfil needs and wants, you should also ensure that this was done at a profit.

The second phase had two significant effects on the marketing scene. First, it meant that product development took centre stage in many companies' marketing departments. After all, if you want to fulfil customer wants and needs, what better way than developing new products. And, in the heyday of growing markets in the 1960s this was the right fuel for a successful business. For instance, at this time in the United States, 90% of consumer markets were growing and providing plenty of opportunities for identifying new needs.

Second, the focus on better understanding of the customers meant that segmentation became a key subdiscipline to marketing. To best understand a customer group you need to segment and define the common parameters of the group, so that you can best fulfil their needs. Both the new product development focus and segmentation were very successful techniques in a growing market where demand was still unsatisfied. The understanding that you have to satisfy customer needs and wants in order to be successful was something good business people had always understood. But the advent of modern marketing meant that this now had a theoretical and even academic backing and, more importantly, methods were developed to better understand the customers and what they would like to have.

The third phase began in the 1980s as the customer adaptation strategy on its own was not sufficient any more. Competition was increasing in virtually all sectors, and demand started to tail off. There were no longer, at least in the developed markets, any unfulfilled needs; instead, there were a great number of suppliers with products and services of increasingly higher quality. In addition, particularly in consumer goods markets, the growth was no longer present. Instead of 90% of markets being in a growth phase as in the 1960s, by the 1980s 90% were stagnating. In such an environment there is only one way forward in order to be successful: you have to be better than everyone else. The concept of constant improvement, *kaizen*, was turned into the key success factor also from a marketing point of view and not only as a manufacturing technique. In marketing, *kaizen* means constant improvement of product and service quality, constant improvement in the perceived values of the brands, constant improvement in the efficiency of the company and constant pressure on being better than the 'other' brands.

Another difference between the second and third phase is that while in the former case the focus was on getting customers to try the product or service, adapting the product so that the customer would buy, in the latter case the focus is on retaining customers. Customer retention is very important for most businesses. Although few studies have truly verified the effect on profits from increases in loyalty, a couple of studies indicate that a 5% increase in loyalty has produced profit increases of somewhere between 20% and 50%. In most instances the vast majority of the business is repeat purchases, so commonsense says that if you can have a high repeat purchase rate you save on recruiting new customers, which all adds up to higher profits.

With this focus on attracting demand, being seen as better than competition whatever or whoever this might be, we also have increasing efforts in concept marketing. The product or service on its own is, of course, no longer enough to attract the

---

## Example

One by now almost classical example of this is the UK soft drink Tango. Tango was until 1992 a traditional orange sparkling soft drink, the kind you will find in most countries around the world (such as Fanta and Orangina). The brand was launched in the 1950s and in 1986 it was acquired by Britvic – a leading UK drinks company. Until the early 1990s when the brand was relaunched sales were acceptable but not brilliant at 1 million cans per day.

Soft drinks marketing pre-Tango was almost without exception in the 'Coca-Cola' style, i.e. beautiful young people having a good time, feeling refreshed by drinking the brand being advertised.

With Tango a totally different approach was taken, using street-credible British humour in a visually dramatic and very funny way, for the first time in UK soft drinks advertising. Sales responded and from being a soft drink 'me-too' brand Tango became a distinct, strong and leading brand. During the first year with the new advertising, the revitalized brand increased sales by 30% and today Tango is the sixth best selling soft drink in the country with take home sales of over £100 million, ahead of brands such as Schweppes and 7-up.

interest of the customers in a crowded market place. A real concept is required, one that can lift the mundane to a higher level, make the brand and the offering really interesting.

The success formula for the third phase is simple: ensure that you are better than the others. The implementation is difficult as it requires a thorough understanding of the customers, the competition and the ability of the company to provide superior products. While we all tend to think that the current situation is the most difficult and that the people in the past do not have much to teach us – a very common attitude in marketing departments – I would like to issue a warning.

In order to excel as a marketing executive you need to master *all* three phases. From the first phase you need to learn to understand and be able to implement all different types of sales promotions and other marketing tools. Not only in order to correctly and cost-effectively market the products and services developed by the company according to the principles of the next two phases, but also for the very simple reason that I have yet to come across a company that does not, from time to time, find itself in a situation where it is necessary to 'push sales'.

From the second phase one has to adapt the principle of fully understanding the customers and develop products and services that are really needed. A detailed and creatively analysed study of not only the customers' needs and wants, but also the behaviour, values and aspirations, is necessary in order to succeed. This will all, however, come to nothing if the marketed offer is not seen as superior to competition, the final hurdle to gain strength in the market place.

# 3
# The importance of being Number 1

Depending on one's outlook being Number 1 might seem the most obvious thing in the world, or totally unnecessary. In the former case, please skip to the next chapter, for others, please read on as being, or aspiring to be, Number 1 is an essential part of a successful brand development strategy.

This is not only a belief and a way of life. The fact is that the market position influences the profitability, a statement which is supported by several different research reports, from the PIMS data base to academic studies. The increasing pressure on business has meant that in most market sectors there is only room for a market leader, a second and perhaps a third supplier if they manage to differentiate themselves away from Number 1. Any other competitors are bound to have to compete on a 'pure' price platform which is unlikely to be successful as the volumes will be below that of the market leader.

From this follows that only brands that are Number 1 or aspire to be Number 1 have a future, and any executive with a less ambitious target is doing his/her company a disservice. If you are less than Number 1, you are a follower with no ambition to win. Such a mentality is too weak to survive in a business environment that is getting increasingly competitive and even hostile.

The mentality in market leading companies is, as a rule, very different from the one in companies struggling at the bottom of the brand pile. If you are leading, you are respected by your suppliers and customers, you have the opportunity to think ahead as you already know what is working today. The companies behind have first to catch up with the leader before they can think of overtaking. This is one reason why so few companies succeed in beating market leaders head-on. If a company manages to overtake the Number 1 this is usually due to either the challenger outsmarting the leader in using new channels (such as Dell computers), new products (quartz watches) or new ways of doing business (IKEA – the home furnishing retailer). Otherwise in most situations change of leadership in a market only take place if the market leader makes some serious mistakes, such as the British motorbike industry in the post-war period.

The position of being Number 1 is one of immense strength and is a tremendous asset. Many brand leading companies, accustomed to being Number 1, often do not fully appreciate this and do not use it sufficiently actively in achieving market targets. Being Number 1 covers at least two different aspects. The first one, and the most difficult to achieve, is to be Number 1 in the mind of the current and potential customers. The second one is to be Number 1 in the market place, in physical terms being the most important supplier of goods and/or services.

## FIRST IN WHAT?

Being first does not mean that you have to be the biggest. It might mean that your brand is the preferred brand in a certain part of a city, in a specialized sector of the market or just in doing one particular task, such as customer service. The definition as such does not matter as long as it is relevant to the market and the company. However, it is essential that the product category or market sector is defined properly. This key point will be covered in greater detail later in the book.

## FIRST CHOICE IN THE MIND

Being first in the mind of the customers, current and potential, means that you are the obvious choice. Say 'refreshing soft drink' and most think Coca-Cola, say 'cigarettes' and most say Marlboro, say 'traditional luxury cars' and most say Rolls-Royce and to move outside of consumer goods, say 'aircraft' and most will think of Boeing. The brand that is first in the mind is the brand that gets the highest recognition – is the brand that comes first on the 'shopping list' whether the shopping list is one of a country buying nuclear reactors or a housewife doing the weekly shopping.

IBM was once the obvious choice for a computer – regardless of what type. This position to be the obvious choice in the computer market does not exist any more. The loss of leadership has meant that not only is IBM a less profitable and more vulnerable competitor, the market definition has changed with it. Today's obvious choices are Microsoft for PC software, Intel for PC processors, AppleMac (at least still at the time of writing) for graphics and IBM for large computers. The benefits of being the obvious choice are enormous. You are known, you are short-listed, at least in the mind of the buyer, and the distribution channels think they need your brand.

How to achieve becoming Number 1 in the mind is one of the crucial aspects of brand development and is covered in Part 3. The subject is raised already at this stage as the mental attitude of being, or want to be, Number 1 is, in my view, crucial to successful brand development.

## FIRST CHOICE IN THE MARKET

While being the first in the mind has some very important advantages, being first in the market also carries some tangible benefits. Of course the two go together but there are brands with limited market presence who still command a Number 1 position in the mind. In the UK for instance virtually everybody regards Marks & Spencer as the leading retailer but M&S is not the biggest in the market, that honour goes to Tesco. A more extreme example is that Ferrari is the first in the mind when it comes to super sports cars but the market sector is so small that there are no tangible benefits from this position. It is also correct to state that some of the advantages under this heading are not strictly tied to being Number 1, it is tied to being big.

Although the market trends in general are towards more and more market segments and a more fragmented market place, the fact remains that in most markets big is beautiful. For instance in the FMCG sector Professor Ehrenberg of London South Bank Business School and his colleagues have proved that without doubt the most important factor for a brand to be successful is to be big. If you are big, you are chosen more often than Number 2 or 3 in the market sector. It is to a degree a circular argument which can leave any executive frustrated but the fact remains: the most important factor to bear in mind when you want to be Number 1 is to be Number 1.

## There are numerous aspects tied to being very big

Traditional business theory says that there are great economies of scale in manufacturing. A big factory is usually more economic to run than a small one; a principle Heinz UK has used to the full in achieving cost-effectiveness in the manufacturing of food products. But it applies to other sectors as well. A big airline is usually more efficient than a small one, they can utilize the aircraft more effectively and run a more effective aircraft maintenance service. This is one reason for British Airways being one of the world's most profitable airlines.

The manufacturing perspective is limiting and only covers part of the real benefits of being big. Supply management carries significant benefits of scale. Ford can buy parts for their cars cheaper than Volvo, just as a large supermarket will get better terms from suppliers than the small corner store.

Distribution is also an activity with significant scale effects. Storage and stock control systems are relatively cheaper the bigger you are. For an airline, the booking system is virtually a fixed cost and only a large airline can afford its own system – again benefits of scale. These effects often override classical marketing theory. The big supermarket does not fulfil customer needs for prime cuts of beef as well as the local butcher but the supermarket certainly has the upper hand in value for money due to the scale effects.

These are all tangible and well-recognized effects but the marketing effects can be as dramatic. To advertise a small brand costs the same as advertising a big one. To produce a commercial or even a company brochure costs the same, regardless of size of the brand. Developing a strong brand, the intellectual capacity and capital required is the same for a small brand as a big one. These are very important factors in understanding why it makes sense to have big brands and why big brands with a less exact fit to customer needs often succeed against very targeted, but smaller, brands. For instance Disney does not always fulfil the exact needs of the audience, but the sheer power behind the development of the products is of such a scale that more targeted films by other family film producers are totally dwarfed.

All of the major international FMCG companies take advantage of this situation. Unilever, Nestlé, Procter & Gamble, General Foods/ Kraft-Jacobs-Suchard, Mars and many others have, over time, made great use of their ability to leverage the intellectual brand equity across continents and as such achieved higher profitability.

### GETTING TO THE TOP – A WARNING

Casual study of market research data can lead to the conclusion that if only the company and the brand is Number 1, everything will be all right. This is of course not true. The brand leader position is an *effect* of 'doing the right things', not the reason, so a strategy built on expansion at all costs is unlikely to succeed.

The Swedish ball-bearing company SKF has long had a strategy of market dominance, so far with limited success from a profitability point of view as, apparently, the volume objective has dominated over leveraging and developing a brand approach.

The Number 1 position, in order to be sustainable, must be built on a solid foundation of perceived product and/or service superiority and a brand process to ensure top of mind.

# 4

# Brand management – creating preference

Brand management is at the core of any business activity as brands are all around us and all companies, more or less successfully and more or less deliberately, manage the reputation and the values tied to their name and symbols.

Brand management is only occasionally carried out by brand managers. Brand managers in the European sense of the word are fairly junior people who are entrusted with developing and implementing marketing activities for a specific brand, or range of product and services under a brand. The true management of the brand in these situations is usually carried out by more senior managers, such as marketing managers and directors. This is not to devalue the very important function of brand managers; a good brand manager can make a lot of difference to a brand. Their main role is in most cases not to strategically manage the brand but to 'make things happen', drive the brand forward through an intelligent mix of different marketing activities and persuading other company functions to focus on the brand in his/her charge.

As the value of a brand is created by all the different activities the customer will connect with the brand, the brand management process is identical to managing all the factors that are externally apparent and relates to the brand, i.e. virtually all the activities of the company. In this we include, of course, the more obvious aspects such as the product and/or service itself and marketing communication, but we must also include all other possible contacts with the company. This includes any sales personnel such as travelling representatives and order takers at the head office, receptionists, switchboard operators, delivery personnel, even all employees who might, even if they work in the factory, meet customers and influence the perception of the brand. In a service organization this is even more pronounced as the brand is primarily represented by all the people in the customer interface, usually the vast majority of the employees. Some aspects of the company's activities are, of course, more important than others, but every little bit matters. This is why brand management is an issue for senior management, not the brand manager.

Successful brand management focuses on creating preference, ensuring that the products and/or services sold under the brand's umbrella of values really are perceived as superior to those of the competitors; and that these products and services really offer the best perceived value for money possible. It is just like running a pub or a bar; to be successful you have to be better than the pubs next to you. In that way the customers will come to you and not the other place. In the current business climate there is only one way of ensuring this happens and it is to constantly work on improving the value perception, to maximize the perceived value within the operational opportunities and constraints of the business.

When a brand represents superior value for money, the company has a distinct competitive advantage. It is essential to remember that the value for money proposition has to be delivered cost-effectively! If not, there is no competitive advantage, no sustainable value proposition and no long-term brand platform. The link to the symbol, the brand, has of course to be very clear and distinct, otherwise the competitive advantages have no identity and the customers no chance of finding the products and services (see Figure 4.1).

## Example

One excellent example is Andrex toilet tissue in the UK. Andrex was originally a brand for gentlemen's disposable handkerchiefs sold only at Harrods, London. In its more modern incarnation as a brand for toilet tissue it was launched by Bowater-Scott in 1956 and became the brand leader in 1962, where it has remained.

The brand promise is centred on three crucial words, soft, strong and long and since 1972 this has been communicated with the help of Golden Labrador puppies – one of the best recognized and loved advertising symbols in the country. All through the life of the brand, the strength of the brand proposition has been communicated through media and product enhancement, with a number of changes to the product to make it more and more appealing.

During the 1980s the brand managed to more-or-less keep its share of the market despite a general trend towards more and more retailer own label products. In addition Scott managed during this period to build a much larger premium sector in the toilet tissue market in the UK than in other Western European countries.

The case of Andrex is however not without problems. In the early 1990s the brand was apparently starved on product innovation and a couple of years into the decade, Andrex started to lose share to own label and competition, from around 30% to almost 20%.

The brand was saved by being sold to the main competitor Kimberley-Clark and the new brand owners are once again investing in making the product even softer and stronger, illustrated in the commercials with young children and Labrador puppies playing with the tissue. At the time of writing, the brand is back on the growth track with sales up 10% in 1997 (A C Nielsen/*Checkout* magazine).

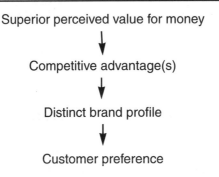

Superior perceived value for money

Competitive advantage(s)

Distinct brand profile

Customer preference

**Figure 4.1**  *Linking superior value and customer preference*

The difference between a company that manages this process actively and one that relies on *ad hoc* activities and the goodwill of its customers, is that the former will have a brand profile that is distinct, consistent and built on a solid foundation which will lead the brand to be trusted and remembered; while in the latter case the fortunes of the company are at the mercy of the competitors. There will also, in this case, be a brand profile, but not one that is managed. The perceptions of the brand can be totally inconsistent with the objectives of the company and even be so weak that any significant competitive threat will undermine the company's future.

Entrepreneurial organizations have an advantage in this respect. Such an organization is usually so influenced by the founder's personality that there (indirectly) is a very consistent brand profile in everything the company does. Richard Branson's Virgin Atlantic is a typical example with a consistent profile in how the staff presents itself, how the publicity is generated and how the airline is managed. All these aspects are influenced by Richard Branson's personality. The entrepreneurial model does have its limitations. It appears that the Virgin group's efforts to run railways in the UK has run into difficulties, as the Virgin railways company has not been able to live up to the expected customer service level.

The brand building process is a total process, involving all aspects of a company. The internal focus of the process cannot be ignored, it is important in creating the foundation from which all external activities can be built, so that regardless of who or what in the company is in contact with the customers they will represent the brand. Consequently the only real brand manager in a company is the person ultimately responsible for the brand, usually the Chief Executive or Divisional Director.

## SETTING OBJECTIVES

Brand management will not be successful unless specific targets are set, in this respect it is no different from any other management process. To build a brand one has to review three levels of targets (see Figure 4.2).

Business objectives

Marketing objectives

Communication objectives

***Figure 4.2*** *Three levels of targets*

The business objectives are set for the company as a totality and would cover elements such as profits and growth. The marketing objectives refer to what the marketing function has to achieve and aspects directly related to the market such as brand share, position in defined market segments or whatever is appropriate to the situation. The communication objectives are related to what the brand communication can influence, such as awareness and attitudes.

For brand management to be cost-effective the communication objectives need, of course, to be consistent with the marketing objectives which in turn must fit the business objectives. All this might seem very simple and straightforward, which it is, but the different objectives often get muddled which can, for instance, make follow up and accountability difficult to assess. As an example, if communication objectives include a marketing objective such as increasing brand share, the advertising and PR will have an impossible task and if they succeed, these activities will only be part of the reason.

# 5
# Value-added marketing

In my book *Value-added Marketing – Marketing Management for Superior Results* (McGraw-Hill 1992) I defined the role of marketing as

> to constantly improve the perceived relative value
> for money of the company's products.

This is still, and probably always will be, the role of marketing in a successful company. A company that strives to add value to its products and services will build a long-term business through the perceived superiority of its brands.

The understanding of the concept of value-added marketing is crucial to successful marketing. Other people might well use a different terminology but the end result of effective marketing is that whatever is being supplied is seen by the customers, current and potential, as superior to what other companies are offering. Value-added marketing is not replacing the traditional marketing concept of satisfying customer needs and wants, it is building on it, taking it one step further as described in the previous chapter on the three phases of marketing.

Value-added marketing consists of two different parts, the reality and the perception. Much has been written and said about the power of perception, but it is my firm view based on observing numerous companies that a brand platform that is built on perception alone will not survive in the longer term. The perception has to rest on a solid foundation of real product and/or service superiority; this applies to all products and services, although to different degrees. A tin of baked beans and a bottle of perfume will both require the two aspects but of course not to the same extent.

This is – again in my personal view – not only a business issue, although those arguments are powerful enough in their own right, it is also a moral one. We as marketing executives have a responsibility towards society not only to present our products and services truthfully but to ensure that we strive constantly towards providing something better, improving society. If not, people will mistrust our claims, which will be to the detriment of everyone; and in the end we will be overtaken by other companies who will be seen as trusting and honest. So, whether we take the moral high ground or not, from a commercial point of view there is no alternative but to ensure that what we do is ethically sound. However, this does not mean you have to be boring or that you should present your wares in any other way but the most attractive. Our duty as marketers is also to make the most of what we have, taking the arguments and presenting them to the best of our ability.

This reality is, however, not worth anything at all if it is not appreciated by the customers, and this is where the skills of the marketing executive comes into play. Product and service benefits can be presented in such a boring way that no one will notice, or against such a backdrop of bad imagery that no one will believe the sender.

While a bad perception and good product is a recipe for bad business, an excellent perception and poor product is no better. The difference is that in the latter case there will be some initial interest but the repeat purchase rate will in due course kill off the business. In today's business world there are not that many relevant examples of this as most companies have come to realize that there is not much point in selling substandard products and services. A more classic example is the US automobile industry in the 1960s and early 1970s, when poor product quality hidden behind glossy advertising and chrome filled car designs left the market place wide open for first European imports such as the Volkswagen Beetle and then later all the Japanese cars.

> ## *Example*
>
> During 1996/97 the British railway system was privatized. British Rail had a reputation which was less than flattering – a situation not unusual in the European railway business. The passengers, and everyone else as well, were convinced that British Rail ran a poor service with constant delays – never mind the reality. When the privatized companies took over, there were in several instances great expectations. Passengers expected a change for the better, that the railways would change the way British Airways had changed when it was privatized in the early 1980s. Unfortunately the expectations regarding the railways were not instantly fulfilled, the new railway companies were as bad or even worse than British Rail because in reality British Rail's punctuality was not that bad, it was mainly a perception of delays. The marketing of British Rail had failed to communicate the real standards of travel while the new companies apparently failed to recognize the management skills required in running an efficient railway – perhaps suffering from the same misconceptions regarding the past as the vast majority of passengers.

However there are market segments where the reality is still way behind the attempts to create a favourable perception. In most Western countries banks and other financial institutions tell us through their advertising how wonderful they are despite providing a service which is rather poor; the poor delivery has made the marketing communication a waste of time. One of the few effective marketing activities in the financial sector in the UK in recent years was when NatWest, under their then new marketing director Raoul Pinnell, decided to cut all advertising and put the money saved into staff training: improving the service so that it could live up to any claims made in the advertising.

For effective marketing the perception has to be backed by reality. There is no point in trying to create a favourable perception for a product or service which is substandard. Similarly there is no point in having a superior product or service if the market place does not recognize the benefits. Value-added marketing is about ensuring that the reality is in place, that the market place recognizes these benefits and that the emotional, or abstract, dimensions of the offer are built to a superior level. It is

by building all these variables into a strong proposition, symbolized by a distinct brand, you win in the market place.

---

## *Example*

Nike is one of the most admired brands in the world. Today it is not
only a very strong brand in itself, but also a brand and a company that
has managed to transform the sport shoes market, once at the very
bottom of the footwear ladder with no fashion element whatsoever, to
a market where customers are prepared to pay high premiums.

The $9 billion sales and universal recognition of the 'swoosh' brand
symbol did, however, not happen without considerable effort, focus,
creativity and other marketing skills. The values of the brand were created over time by elements such as creating a demonstrable product
advantage in the waffle sole, a constant flow of attractive product
designs to demonstrate that the shoe was a fashion item; and exciting,
appealing and relevant communication, often with the help of sports
personalities.

The building of the brand is coupled with a determined policy of finding
the most cost-effective product sourcing to ensure that funds are available
for product and design development as well as brand communication.

---

# 6
## Understand!

Time and time again it becomes apparent that an essential part of successful marketing, regardless of approach, is to understand all aspects of the market. Traditionally the focus has been single-minded on understanding the customer, but this is not enough. In addition to understanding the customers and the market dynamics, you also need to have a thorough appreciation of the competition and, not least, your own company's capabilities.

### THE MARKET

A traditional market analysis will cover, at least, market size, growth rates, important subsegments and an overview of the market dynamics. The hard facts are important to get 'a fix' on the magnitude of the market segment, how it is moving forward, what is important, etc.

Understanding the market is not only important from the point of view of providing a backdrop to the marketing strategy; it is also important in order to be on the same level as the customers. The customers have often been operating in the market for a long time and they know what has happened, they know the successes and failures of the past, and to be a credible supplier you need to be seen as having at least the same depth of understanding.

Reviewing the past, and in particular the immediate past, will also build an awareness of what it is that drives a particular sector forward. There are obvious answers such as style driving the fashion market or processing capacity driving the PC market but also others such as recipe adaptations building business in the frozen ready meals market; or the late spring weather influencing the sales of ice cream impulse items in Northern Europe. Many companies hold this information only in an unstructured format. A document with the key aspects of the hard facts written down, as well as a brief analysis of the dynamics, will help in creating common ground in the company to understand the market place.

## THE COMPETITION

One main objective of value-added marketing is to be perceived as better than competition. In order to be able to be better you have to know what the competition stands for. Also in this respect a systematic approach is advisable. Understanding the competition includes defining who the competition is; why the competitors are in this market; what their strengths and weaknesses are; range of products and services; what their market position is; brand positioning; marketing support, etc.

Over the last decade in the consumer goods market the initiative in many market sectors has moved from the traditional FMCG manufacturers to the retailers. One reason for this, in my view, is the more pronounced competitive focus in the retail trade. Most successful retailers, if not all, from Sainsbury's and Wal-Mart to IKEA and ALDI keep a very close eye on the competitive situation, monitoring the prices, the advertising, the range, the location, the consumer profile and every other aspect of the competition on a regular basis.

Competitive monitoring is not a luxury in today's marketing battle, it is a necessity. If resources are limited at least follow systematically all published material and if appropriate use the products and services of competition on a regular basis. Not every company can do what the car industry has been doing for decades, buying several competitive models and taking them apart to learn from competition; but collecting brochures, competitive advertising and reading the financial pages, as well as the appointments section, is something anyone can do.

## CAPABILITIES

Every marketing executive knows that it is important to understand the market, the customers, and increasingly the competition. Based on our own experience from seminars and consulting there are still not many who fully understand the importance of 'know thyself'.

A study of business start-ups in the United States showed that many businesses failed after about four years. The reason, according to the study, was that by then most founders had lost track of what really had made the business a success and consequently no longer took care of the original competitive edge. If asked 'why are you successful' many companies give a superficial answer in the style of 'we offer excellent quality to an attractive price'. That is not to define the core capabilities of a company.

Professor John Kay published in 1993 an excellent study called 'Foundations of Corporate Success', a detailed study of successful companies. He concluded, not surprisingly, that companies were successful due to their core capabilities which he classified in four different categories:

- Architecture – how the companies 'do things'.

- Reputation – in marketing terms the strength of the brands.

- Innovation – how innovative in the wider sense of the word the companies are.

- Strategic assets – what assets the companies have which give them an 'unfair' advantage, such as the monopoly to distribute letters for the Post Office in the past or the existence of favourable purchasing channels.

The four categories of capabilities can be one way of structuring the analysis of the company's capabilities and deciding what capabilities are relevant to a specific brand. John Kay also concluded that the 'will' to achieve something as expressed in mission statements and the like were of very limited use unless they were strongly related to the capabilities of the company. This might seem obvious but is often forgotten.

---

## *Example*

Scandinavian Airlines was one of many airlines that during the 1980s decided that its business was not air travel but 'the travel experience' and as such the company should provide not only air travel but also credit card and charter companies. These businesses are quite different from running an airline and apparently Scandinavian Airlines lacked the key capabilities in running them profitably. The end effect was that resources were wasted; management lost the focus on providing excellent air travel and the ambitions to become a leading European carrier were never fulfilled. Today the airline is back to its focus but as a regional airline relying on a partnership with Lufthansa to service the world.

---

There are many other similar examples such as Daimler-Benz's (makers of Mercedes-Benz) objective in the late 1980s to become a leading technology group which almost led the company into bankruptcy; and Volvo's ambition in the late 1970s to become a 'leisure' company which led to a dilution of profitability and management focus. Both examples are a sharp contrast to the focused approach of BMW. This 'other' German company was a small car manufacturer close to ruin in the late 1950s. Due to a distinct and focused approach closely tied to the key capabilities of the company it is today a leading and very profitable company. It has also in the process developed into Europe's, if not the world's, leading brand builder in the car industry.

Defining the capabilities of the company from the perspective of the brand is an essential part of building the foundations for competitive branding. Building a brand cannot be done in isolation from the capabilities of the company. A claim and strategy must have a foundation in something the company is excellent at; otherwise there will be no competitive advantage and ultimately no reason for a customer to choose the brand as another brand will be more suitable to deliver on the promise.

## THE CUSTOMERS

It is a 'motherhood statement' to say that effective marketing requires excellent understanding of the customers. All effective marketing is built on a foundation of understanding the customer, who they are, what their aspirations and problems are, etc. The methods used to understand the customers better rank from close scrutiny of internal data (often neglected) to extensive market research programmes. Excellent literature is available on this subject so it will not be covered here.

---

*Example*

An ambitious project to understand the customers better was part of the revival of Scandinavian Airlines. One element involved videoing passengers during the various stages of their air travels. More than 1,400 hours of film was recorded plus 230 hours of direct personal observations. (NB The filming was made with the agreement of the passengers.)

---

For competitive branding two specific aspects of understanding the customers require highlighting. The first one is the importance of personal dialogue with the customers. It is striking that virtually all successful entrepreneurs talk to customers on a regular basis; this is particularly pronounced in retailing. Lord Sainsbury, who built Sainsbury's to become the leading retailer in the UK, and Sir Ian MacLaurin, who for many years led Tesco and turned it into a leading quality operator overtaking Sainsbury's in 1996, both toured the stores and spoke to customers and frontline staff as part of their regular schedule. Ingvar Kamprad, founder of IKEA – the home furnishing retailer – is still today a frequent visitor to IKEA stores around the world, talking to people to understand better what is going on.

Although one has to be careful not to draw far-reaching conclusions from a personal dialogue with a couple of customers, the discipline of meeting 'real' customers regularly will provide a perspective that no formal market research in the world can give. It is, however, not a substitute for quantifiable research programmes, it is a complement.

The other aspect is the use of customer data to understand the customers better. All companies have different forms of customer data, usually structured either on the basis of invoicing or accounting principles. Although this information can be surprisingly useful, the power of computing means that a much more sophisticated approach can be taken if information is collected in the 'proper' way.

The most obvious example is the promotional or 'loyalty' store cards. The store cards' data are mines of information in that they track the exact purchasing pattern of individuals. The cards can link this to personal information collected when the card is issued and it can be updated by tracking the consumer as he/she is exposed to different marketing initiatives. While the store cards can be excellent promotional tools, real additional value of the cards will lie in the data base and the opportunity the data base provides to really understand actual consumer behaviour, not 'claimed' as in most market research nor statistical snapshots as in consumer panels but actual hard data.

The principle of the store card does not apply only to retailers. It obviously applies to wholesalers in business-to-business situations and, actually, to *all* companies with a direct link to the customers. The effective use of transaction data, effectively structured and followed, can provide amazing insights into customer behaviour, giving the user an additional opportunity for building competitive brands. The subject is also covered in 'Direct marketing' in Part 3.

Understanding the market, the competition, the capabilities and the customers is crucial to success. Analysing and applying the information available will become even more important in the future as data processing power continues to become more and more available. To attempt to build a brand without (a) having done the homework in understanding all these aspects, and (b) having a programme in place to follow up on the activities, is a waste of time and effort. It is like building a house on quicksand instead of on a concrete foundation.

## SUMMARY OF PART 1

The role of marketing has moved from only satisfying customer needs and wants to ensuring that a brand is perceived by the customers as superior to competition.

The role of brand management is to manage this process cost-effectively, so that the brand is first in the mind and first in the market, the reward for creating customer preference. To achieve this brand management needs to fully understand not only the customers and the market place but also competition and the capabilities of the organization.

# Part 2
## Competitive brand development

# INTRODUCTION

Why do we have brands and why do we take an interest in ensuring that the brands are as strong as possible? For one simple reason, to allow us to compete more effectively.

The brand development process is not one that has come out of academic research, it is a process that has been developed over time by practitioners from various strands of the business world. We have seen what has worked, and has not; we have developed new ideas and concepts, sometimes successfully and sometimes not. It has been a process of trial and error which has over time built up a bank of knowledge which we now can tap into.

This whole process has meant that we now know more about how to develop brands and the likelihood of success is higher if we follow at least some of these straightforward 'rules' and processes. However, as the environment is constantly changing and not one situation is identical to another we can never be sure of success regardless of how well we manage the process, nor can we be sure that the competitor who ignores all rules and processes will not get it right.

Part 2 will cover a model for building brands, some key expressions and concepts as well as advice and examples of effective and competitive brand building, all of which hopefully will make it easier for you to successfully manage the brand development process for competitive branding.

# 1
# Why branding?

Much of what we do is considered self-evident and is not questioned. In today's marketing world it takes a very brave, and perhaps foolish, person to question whether or not one should brand a product/service. Even if the answer is a distinct 'yes' we should still consider the question as the answer will tell us why we should spend time and money on branding; and also ensures that we do not forget the objective of the exercise.

It is a fundamental business truth that a company or brand will not succeed unless it has a perceived competitive advantage. You have to be seen as better than the competition in one or several aspects, as otherwise there are no reasons for a customer to choose you instead of the alternatives, or indeed to spend any money at all.

It is not enough to have a competitive advantage, you have to be seen as having the advantage. A potential advantage is not of any use unless the customers can identify you as the supplier and/or the product. If there are no means of identification, you cannot be seen as having an advantage as this will not be visible to the public. Fairly simple and obvious, but an essential part of the branding rationale.

The brand takes the role of identifying the product. With the help of a brand, the customers can not only see you and talk about you, they can also remember you. The brand is the means by which you can differentiate your offering from that of everyone else, it is the way to signal that this is the product that has all the advantages the customer is looking for. It is of course not necessary to have a brand in the modern sense. If your product is sufficiently good, people will find ways of branding your product and services. However, it is much easier to describe your favourite restaurant as 'The Mill House' instead of saying that 'My favourite restaurant is the one in a white, old building, situated by the river and it has a large waterwheel, which used to be part of an old mill, in the middle . . . etc.'

---

### *Example*

Even in a business such as properties there are companies that manage to establish a brand. Paul Reichmann, the Canadian-based developer of properties such as Battery Park City in New York, Canary Wharf in London and One Canada Place in Toronto, is regarded as a property megabrand. With a claim to 'change the face of cities', Reichmann adds to the perceived quality of the property which in turn leads to higher rents.

---

The first and most basic function of the brand is to cost-effectively identify a product or service. With the name you differentiate Coca-Cola from Pepsi-Cola, Marlboro from Camel and Volvo from Mercedes.

---

### *Example*

If a brand does not exist, and there are distinct product advantages, people will find ways of differentiating. The following story has been reported from the former Soviet Union where all television sets carried the same brand name but were manufactured in different factories although apparently each factory operated to a different standard. As the sets were expensive, care was taken when investing in one. After a while it became fairly common knowledge that sets with a certain sequence in the serial number on the back of the set came from a specific factory. This piece of information only became relevant when people also discovered that sets from one factory were of a higher quality than those from another.

The result was that customers would look out for sets with this specific set of numbers and try to buy these sets in preference to others. The number sequence became the real brand, not the name on the front of the set.

---

In short, the brand is a short-cut in the communication process. With a name, a brand, follows a full set of impressions and emotions. If you are in the UK and mention the name Margaret Thatcher everyone over the age of twelve will be able to picture an individual and emotions, positive and/or negative, will emerge. Similarly, in the US the name Ronald Reagan, or in more recent years Bill Clinton, will set off in the mind a plethora of impressions. This not only applies to politicians who in many respects are becoming more and more managed like traditional brands but also artistes and other famous people. 'Magic' Johnson, Mick Jagger, Michael Jackson, Princess Diana and perhaps the Spice Girls are all words that represent individuals who generate an impression in the minds of the public. They are brands, in some respects due to personal achievements, in others due to skilful manipulation of the media. But in all instances the mention of the name will allow rapid, and thus cost-effective, communication of a number of values and impressions. It only takes a second or perhaps even just a fraction of a second.

This role, the ability to trigger a set of 'stored' values in the minds of the customers, is an important one for the brand. That is why we are developing brands, so that we can tap into the customers' ability to retain impressions and link them to a visual or oral expression.

## BRANDING – THE EXPRESSIONS

The word branding is in itself sometimes the cause of some confusion and even misunderstandings as to what brand development is really all about. The reason is that it is being used fairly carelessly in respect of two different types of activities. On the one hand it is used to describe the graphical or 'artistic' execution of a brand identity, i.e. the shape and form of the logo, the design of corporate literature and letter heads etc., and on the other hand the term refers to the building of values represented by the brand.

In the context of this book it is only the latter definition that is being used as that is, in my view, what real branding is about. This is not to say that the graphical execution of a brand profile is not important. A strong visual profile can do a lot of good for a brand, but the process used to build a visual profile is very different from that of building strong brand values. Essentially all you have to do is to brief a good design agency, of which there are many, and once the profile is defined implement the programme with all the skills and attention to detail that is required.

To build real brands you need to build strong values. It is by having strong values linked to your brand that the brand will have commercial power and stay in the minds of the customers for a long time.

Many companies unfortunately mix the concepts. More than once a 'new brand profile' is being announced with the message that this will change the future of the company, but in reality it is only a new visual programme and once the novelty factor has disappeared, the brand is back to square one.

Examples of this can be found among petrol companies, banks and other financial institutions and some government agencies. In my view BP is a prime example. BP has one of the best executed graphical profiles in the world; a distinct colour scheme, logo and typeface consistently applied, etc. However, there is very little in the form of values tied to the brand. The average petrol customer still chooses a petrol station on the basis of location, not brand, and it is most unusual to come across someone who actually goes out of his/her way to find a specific brand of petrol, unless it is to find a lower price. The effect can be seen in the UK in the form of the significant gain in market share that the large supermarkets have managed to capture with their own label petrol, and in Scandinavia where BP came to a situation where they just sold out their whole operation.

Another example is the rebranding of Pepsi in 1996. The change of colour from red to blue was the object of considerable promotion but the effects on brand share appear to be very limited.

We can also find examples of the reverse, brands with strong values but poor visual identity. One such example is American Express Charge cards, at least in Europe. American Express has still, despite some changes in recent years, a distinct and strong profile as a premium charge card, evident for instance from the fact that a great number of people are prepared to pay a premium to have the card (the annual fee is higher than for most other cards); and retail outlets are prepared to accept a higher cut on American Express purchases than on other cards presumably because the outlets believe that the American Express card holders are more affluent (which they probably are) and that they spend more (again which they perhaps do).

A visual audit of American Express will, however, show that the graphical identity is far from consistent. There are two totally different logotypes, the blue square with the words American Express and the words against a green background as on the card. In addition, on the card you will find two other ways of writing the logo, one with the words 'world service' around a globe, and another on a type of waving banner. And, you have at the centre of the card a picture of a Roman centurion. All in all four different ways of writing the company name, logotypes, and several very different visual impressions.

The BP, Pepsi and American Express examples show that an excellent visual identity will not save a poor identity and a multifaceted visual identity does not necessarily mean that the brand is weak. Even one of the world's strongest brands, Coca-Cola, uses at least three different logos, the traditional one, 'Coke' and a third clearly written one seen at outdoor arenas. There is, however, little doubt that the best way of operating is to have strong values expressed in a distinct visual identity as, for instance, is the case with the car rental companies Hertz and to a degree Avis, airlines such as British Airways and Singapore Airlines and car companies such as BMW and Jaguar.

## WHEN IS A NAME A BRAND?

This is a crucial question for a company. How do you move from having a registered trademark to a brand that generates values and makes people buy the product and service. This process is at the heart of this book and is being dealt with in many different ways. To be able to assess where to start it is important to be aware of the current situation. Of the trademarks and product expressions in the company's portfolio, how many are 'real' brands and how many are just trademarks with perhaps a nice visual profile?

The answer to the question is rarely a straight yes or no. It is for instance a question of degrees and of target groups. While a brand might have a very distinct profile in one part of the market, the same expression might mean nothing at all to others. Magazines read by teenage girls are unknown to most middle-aged men but probably somewhat familiar to girls just outside of the primary target group. Suppliers of nuclear reactors are unknown to most of the public but have a reasonable awareness among nuclear protesters and perhaps people interested in the stock market. While a brand of coffee might be well-established in southern Germany, it might be totally unknown in the rest of Europe; but also in the prime market the non-coffee drinker is unlikely to know it, and the one not doing the shopping and never preparing coffee is again perhaps not that familiar with it.

To simplify matters one can say that a name is a brand if it fulfils the following criteria:

- carries distinct values

- differentiates

- is appealing

- has a clear identity.

The list of criteria is not in rank of importance, they are all important.

A brand represents distinct values, it has a clear profile in the minds of the customers in respect of what it stands for. Coca-Cola is refreshing, Hertz is the leading car rental company and so on. Most brands carry many values and how to create and build these values will be covered in a later chapter. It is easy to test this dimension, just mention the brand name in isolation and see what reaction you get. If the person can describe the brand and come up with expressions which show that this name actually represents any values, the name has passed the test. However, if the answer is a 'blank', then it is just a name, not a brand.

The second aspect of a brand is that it must differentiate, make one product stand out among the rest, be perceived as different from competition. The differentiation aspect is becoming increasingly important in that in most product and service market sectors, there is less and less obvious differentiation and technological break throughs so to stay unique for more than a shorter period of time is increasingly difficult. As an example, many PCs stay differentiated for a very short period of time, because the technology is perceived as being the same and consequently there are very few real brands in this sector.

In a more established sector, such as cars, BMW is clearly seen as different from Volkswagen and also Audi, Mercedes and any other car that aspires to compete in this specific sector. On the other hand it might not be as clear what is differentiating a Daewoo from many other cars other than the sales method employed, i.e. the differentiation is connected to the distribution system and nothing else.

It is appropriate to raise a warning sign in the context of differentiation. It is important to realize that one should not differentiate a brand out of the main stream part of the market sector, in particular if you are a brand leader. It can be tempting for a weak brand leader facing new and tough competition to move the brand to a very special position but in doing so also moving out of the main part of the market. This can be very dangerous as the brand can lose appeal to the majority of customers and becomes a side-lined brand instead of the leading one.

## Example

A glossy women's magazine in a European country had a good position as a premium, generalist, up-market women's magazine. Along came a new editor-in-chief with the brief to make the magazine more attractive, make it stand out among the rest. Through a differentiation process, where the editorial content focused on women's issues in an aggressive way and the magazine got a more extreme fashion profile, the magazine generated a lot of attention, became much more clearly positioned in the market place but in the process lost the main part of the old readership. Fortunately, the old readership was to a large extent replaced by new readers, but the end result was a magazine with lower circulation and a readership which was less loyal and more difficult to satisfy as it was more demanding. No doubt the magazine would have become more profitable with a more gentle face-lift which had allowed it to keep the existing readers while generating new readers in a more gradual way.

The third aspect, appealing, is of course crucial to a brand. There has to be an emotional reason for the customers to trust and rely on this brand. The brand has to be attractive and be a positive experience; successful retailers are often good at fulfilling this requirement. The cosmetics chain Body Shop had, especially in its earlier days, a very dedicated following due to its appealing 'natural' profile. Another retailer with a brand that has very strong appeal is IKEA; dedicated IKEA customers will drive a long distance out of their way to get to an IKEA store.

The final point, identity, is the one that is most easily taken care of and which most brand managers ensure is correctly executed. This said, it is important to appreciate that the brand has to be easily recognized. For instance, in order to brand oranges, you have to put small stickers on each orange, otherwise the customers will not be able to know whether it is Jaffa or Valencia. Similarly, if the customers cannot identity the brand of the product, there is no way you can build brand loyalty. Ralph Lauren's Polo branded clothes would no doubt be less of a success if the brand had been featured only on the label and not on the front of the garment.

Ideally the brand should not only be easy to identify, it should also be easy to remember. A short easily pronounced name is usually better than a complicated one and a distinct visual profile makes the process easier.

Finally, there are occasions when a brand becomes a name. From a branding point of view that is not always a good thing as it can make it not only impossible to protect the use of the name, it makes it very difficult to manage the value profile of the brand. The classical example is Hoover, where the brand is also an everyday expression: 'to Hoover', i.e. to use the vacuum cleaner. In the earlier days of photocopying, people talked about Xeroxing in the same way. In both cases the brand owners are, correctly, fighting all examples of using the brand as a normal word. For instance in dictionaries Hoover is always with capital H, as it is in the spellcheck on the PC I am using to write this book.

---

## *Example*

A more up-to-date example is the Kiwi fruit. The Kiwi fruit is actually called 'Chinese gooseberry' but the New Zealanders growing the fruit, and aiming to market it aggressively, wisely realized that this did not sound very attractive. The decision was taken to rename it and someone came up with the name Kiwi, as in the wingless bird from New Zealand and also a nickname for people from New Zealand. The name and the fruit caught on around the world and all was well; until other countries started to grow the fruit and in some cases, such as Italy, could sell it much more cheaply in Europe. These alternative producers could, and still can, use the Kiwi name as it was not properly registered.

The chosen solution by the farmers in New Zealand having lost the Kiwi brand was to rename their fruit and brand it Zespri, a very expensive exercise and one that will take much expenditure to implement to the level of being a recognized brand expression.

---

The lesson: always ensure that brands are properly registered, don't take anything for granted. Otherwise the brand will become a name and although you will have the glory of having introduced a new word to the world, you will also have lost the opportunity to have a real brand. If you do get into this situation, fight it as Hoover and Xerox have done.

# 2
# The origins of branding – a (very) brief history

If we understand the background to phenomena, or indeed to virtually anything, we are more likely to be able to utilize all the power and possibilities that lie within the concepts. Branding is no different but the purpose here is not to give a full account of the history of branding, as that would fill more than one book, but to give some glimpses of where branding comes from.

The word branding in itself is an indication of why we brand. To brand means literally to burn, i.e. to burn a mark on something, like the farmer or rancher putting his symbol on the cattle with the help of a hot iron. The word itself comes from the Scandinavian word for burning which is 'bränna' and a fire in Swedish is a 'brand'. In other words, to brand is to put one's mark on one's property, or on items one has produced.

Branding as an activity goes back a very long time. According to literature the first example of branding refers to the manufacture of oil lamps in the Greek islands, long before the birth of Christ. Apparently in those days you could buy a primitive form of oil lamp, as in Aladdin, but the quality of the lamp did not show until it had been used as the difference between a good and less good lamp was how long it could be used before falling apart. It was impossible to distinguish between a good and bad lamp at the time of purchase so there was no incentive to make a better lamp. According to the story, one Greek island produced a better, more long-lasting lamp as they had better clay and/or were better craftsmen so they started to mark their lamps with a special symbol. They branded their goods so that they, or the merchant selling the lamps further down the distribution chain, could differentiate the product and, presumably, charge a premium price.

Already this first example illustrates that branding is a method for identifying quality products. Branding is not a useful exercise if your product is identical to all others in the market place, or if you have no desire to set your product apart from the rest. To this I would like to add that based on examples and experience, virtually all products/services can be differentiated and thus have the potential to be branded. I have as yet to come across an example of something that cannot be differentiated.

Moving from antiquity to more modern times we see a number of different ways of branding. Early on hallmarking of gold and silver was introduced and with it usually also the sign of the gold- or silversmith. Branding although of a subtle nature. Another early way of branding was the application of signatures on paintings and furniture by the artists. Rembrandt signed his works of art, as did most other recognized painters, as that was his way of authenticating the painting and thus branding it. Giving it the guarantee that this was the 'real thing'. Antonio Stradivari of Cremona marked his violins so that the buyer would immediately realize who had made the violin and, by implication, that this violin was a superb quality instrument. The 'brand' name Stradivarius became a true premium brand in the stringed instrument market, a position it has kept ever since.

Thomas Chippendale, the eighteenth-century cabinetmaker, was very successful with his furniture, representing at the time an innovative style. In this case not only did Chippendale become a famous brand, the name became synonymous with a specific style. An early example of the Hoover problem described in the previous chapter although in the eighteenth century, before trademark registration became an issue, it was probably seen as the ultimate endorsement.

Up until the middle of the nineteenth century all these branding activities were of a fairly basic type. The artisan marked his goods so that the customers would know who had made it. A sign of confidence, a guarantee and way to build a reputation.

The advent of the railway changed all this. All of a sudden it was possible to transport goods across countries and in the case of the US, across a continent. At the same time we had industrialization, making it possible to efficiently produce goods in factories but in such quantities that you had to sell across a wide area to achieve the necessary volumes. This period saw the rise of the modern branding by the likes of Messrs Procter & Gamble in the US and Lord Leverhulme in the UK. To learn the basics of branding one can do much worse than study the introduction of Ivory soap in the US by Procter & Gamble.

The key to the rise of branding was that all of a sudden the distance between the producer, i.e. the factory and no longer the artisan, and the buyer, the consumer in the city and not the farmer in the country, became much greater. There was no longer any possibility to communicate in person, you had to rely on other means. And the way to do that was to brand the product, i.e. give it a name and a distinct packaging, ensure that the product was always of the same high quality and then use mass communication to tell the public about it. These three elements, identity, quality and communication remains the cornerstones of the branding process although today we have to go into some more detail than 150 years ago.

## BRAND NAMES

The different brand names tell us another part of the story of the evolution of branding. The first brands were names, Rembrandt, Stradivarius, Chippendale, etc. Many of what we now call modern brands are just names. Kraft, Maggi, Heinz, Ford, Nestlé, Guinness are all names of people who founded companies and started selling products which they were proud of. Kellogg's is the perhaps the prime example, in declaring on packs that 'It is not Kellogg's, if it does not say Dr Kellogg's on the pack'. And, it was not just Kellogg's, it was Dr Kellogg's, important in the early days of the brand to boost the health credentials of Dr Kellogg's invention, the cornflake.

Following on from names as brands came companies as brands. BMW (Bayerische Motor Werke) and 3M (Minnesota Mining and Manufacturing Co) are two of the more famous ones but many others exist.

The inventive entrepreneurs of the nineteenth century did not stop, though, at using their own names or company names on the products. Once the power of the brand was recognized, there was a strong incentive to come up with powerful and attractive brand names.

The name Coca-Cola was created by the bookkeeper working for the inventor of the formula. It is a combination of two of the original main ingredients, the coca leaf and the kola nut. An invented name but with strong connections to the origins of the product. Kodak, another classical brand name, is the result of pure imagination. The company founder, George Eastman, wanted a name that was short, powerful and could be registered without problems. He also had an affinity for the letter K. By putting the letter K in the beginning and the end of the word he had a good start. He then just experimented with various combinations until he felt he had a good name.

Names that are totally innovative and bear no relation to existing words are not that common, although we still find examples, in particular when companies are searching for names that can be used across the world. Exxon which replaced Esso (short for Standard Oil) in 1973 is one such example.

Many brand names are devised in order to capitalize on specific values, and this is probably the type of brand names most companies aspire to have to get some help from the name itself to build values. One of the first examples of this is Ivory soap from Procter & Gamble, launched in 1879; the name is a reflection of the white colour of the soap. More recent examples are Flora, the vegetable-based margarine from Unilever, Pampers disposable nappies from Procter & Gamble, Holiday Inn hotels and British Airways' World Traveller for economy intercontinental travelling.

Over time branding has moved from being just a way of identifying the make and a 'seal of guarantee' as Dr Kellogg's, to today's situation where the brand has taken on a more important role as communicator of distinct values.

The on-going theme in all these examples, from the Greek islands onwards, is that the product and service has been branded because the producer is looking for a way of demonstrating that his/her product is better and/or different from all others in the market place. The brand is there to distinguish one product from another, to guarantee a certain quality. This is still at the foundation of brand development. It is a process only worth pursuing if you have a quality product or service – as history tells us.

# 3
## Building brands

This chapter will introduce a model for understanding how brands are created and enhanced. Although the book in its totality is about brand building and development, in this chapter the focus is on how the process actually works, rather than how to do it.

### THE PURCHASING PROCESS

A purchase situation is either a trial, i.e. a first purchase, or a repeat purchase. The way we reach our decision to buy a product or service differs between the two and consequently the marketing mix will differ depending on which of the two is the focus for the brand. In simple terms, to increase penetration the brand needs to invite trial and to build, and keep, business in the longer term the repeat purchase rate must be at a high level.

In a first purchase situation, the customer has to rely totally on communication to decide whether to buy or not. This decision can be an elaborate one as in handling a large building contract or very simple such as deciding what type of soft drink to buy on a hot day. In both cases, assuming that the potential customer has not been supplied before by any of the available alternatives, he/she has to rely on whatever information is available for the decision as he/she will not have any personal experience to fall back on.

Which product to choose will in such a case depend on the

level of *attraction* of the different alternatives. The attraction is a function of communication. It can be due to company communication in the form of brochures, product and service specifications, advertising, PR releases etc. It can also be in the form of third party information. Friends, colleagues, local experts and many others can have voiced an opinion which may have a distinct influence.

Although the attraction brand perception is a function of communication, it is important to remember that the most effective type of communication, personal endorsement, relies on a positive product experience by the endorser (assuming that the individual is not a paid endorser but then it is no longer a 'proper' third party endorsement but sales and advertising).

For a brand to gain new customers it needs to have strong attraction values, potential customers must feel that this brand is superior to others and will provide them with the benefits they are looking for. For the brand to prosper it is essential that the repeat purchase rate is high, or for products unlikely to be bought more than once, that the customers are so satisfied that they will recommend the product or service to someone else.

Successful brand management focuses on building a high repeat purchase rate. The key element in this is to ensure that the brand delivers at least up to the expectations. As in most cases staff in a company tend to overestimate the quality of their own products and services and underestimate the competitors', the company should strive to *over-satisfy* the customers. Perhaps more importantly, in a competitive market, with constant improvements being introduced and new competitors coming in to take market share, it is simply not enough to satisfy customers. To be on the safe side, and also to feel confident that the next time the brand will be chosen, the brand builder should over-satisfy the customers. As mentioned previously, many companies can satisfy a customer but only one can do it the best way. That is why you need to aim for over-satisfaction. A London interior designer once expressed this as 'Never give clients what they want, give them what they never dreamed they could have'.

By over-satisfying the customers they will get a positive impression of the brand, they will feel comfortable with it and be inclined to buy again. For the company, it means higher profitability as it is much more profitable to sell several times to the same, existing customers than to constantly find new ones.

## THE BRAND BUILDING MODEL

Ever since branding was introduced as a distinct activity, academics and practitioners have built models, more or less complicated. The model in Figure 3.1 is introduced as an attempt to describe graphically the branding process in as simple a way as possible.

**Figure 3.1**   *The brand building flow*

The upper part of the model shows that all brands are created in the minds of the customers (the box called 'the Brand') by experiencing the product or service identified with the brand and/or by being influenced by communication. All brand perceptions have their origins in either 'Communication' or 'Experience'.

The process starts by the experience and/or the communication influencing the perception of the brand and then over time brand values will be established. The brand experience does, however, not take place in isolation. If the experience is a positive one, this positive experience will influence the next encounter with the brand in a positive way.

---

*Example*

Nescafé is the leading coffee brand in the UK. If the product is put into a blind test against similar, competitive brands, the product will come out ahead, i.e. be considered as a better coffee by a majority of the consumers. If the same test is carried out but the test is open, i.e. the consumers are aware of the brand, Nescafé of course still comes out as better but with a bigger margin, say rather than the preference rating being 55/45 it might be 65/35. The reason is that the positive experience from previous in-home consumption will positively influence the perception of the coffee taste.

---

As the perception is influenced by previous usage, it becomes important to ensure that each usage situation is a positive experience, thus 'Over-satisfaction'. By over-satisfying the customer he/she will not only be more inclined to use the brand again but also to be more favourably disposed when actually using the brand. In other words, by ensuring a positive experience, the brand owner can create a positive, 'virtuous', circle, where the actual and perceived experiences enforce each other and thus enhance the standing of the brand.

---

*Example*

This has been expressed by Mr Tom Farmer, founder and CEO of Kwik-Fit, a chain of garages specializing in exhaust and tyre repairs, as achieving 'customer delight', not customer satisfaction but delight, and this in one of the least glamorous of industries. That the claim is not just an advertising slogan or a mission statement collecting dust, is verified by an extensive survey programme to measure customers' experience of Kwik-Fit.

---

The Kwik-Fit example is also evidence of the fact that product satisfaction, no 'delight', is even more important in the service industry than when it comes to traditional products. While the product experience for a FMCG brand might account for 75% of the brand experience, for a service industry it is more likely to be 85%.

Most brands are created this way, leaving the communication almost totally out of the circle, certainly at least communication in the classical sense, i.e. advertising. The reason is simple. Very few brands initially have the resources to advertise in an effective way, so there is no alternative to experience-based brand building. For example one of the UK's strongest brands all categories is Marks & Spencer, a brand that has over time received very little advertising support, and a similar example is Body Shop, again a brand with little advertising. In these two cases the visual impact of the shops is, of course, very powerful but at least in the case of M&S a very important part has been played by the quality of staff and merchandise. It is, however, not only in retailing that brands are built without advertising. Many traditional FMCG products have been established with the help of a marketing mix that did not include traditional advertising because the brands could just not afford it.

As indicated communication can be much else other than advertising. Word-of-mouth, i.e. recommendations from friends and trade experts, press articles and, for instance, in retailing, shop front displays and general shop design usually have a much greater impact than traditional advertising. This does not mean, though, that advertising should be ignored, nor that communication should take a back seat, it is a question of getting the perspective right. It is the experience that is the main factor in building the brand, communication comes second. The other reason for putting communication as the second part of the process is that while experience can build a brand on its own, it is highly unlikely that a brand can be built by communication alone, that is by generating interest and brand values through communication and then having it all let down by unsatisfactory experiences. Only con men and travelling salesmen can afford that kind of approach, it is extremely short term.

The role of communication in the brand building process is to enhance the experience. By communicating in an appealing way, the customers will be positively disposed to the brand and the experience will be more positive. The communication works a bit like oil in the brand building works, making it all go smoother, making the building of values quicker. Communication can, of course, also build values in expectation of usage; building values so that the customer will feel inclined to try the product for the first time.

The other part of the formula, once the art was of a sufficiently good quality, was to create awareness and use communication to build the brand. With the help of his manager and art galleries, the name Picasso was spread around the art circles. This was important to create interest but also to reassure buyers of the art. It is a pleasure to buy a nice picture, it is even nicer to realize that you have bought something from an artist about to become famous; and it gives tremendous reassurance to know that the artist whose painting you have just bought is well-established and reviewed in the leading art journals.

---

## *Example*

The brand building model applies not only to traditional brands but also to other brands such as artists. The latter category houses one of the world's most powerful brands, 'Picasso'. Picasso is considered one of the twentieth century's most important painters, his name on a canvas will boost the price to astronomical dimensions. It is a brand with power to transfer values which is way ahead of all consumer goods luxury brands.

It is, however, well worth noting that the Picasso brand was no accident, it was not something that just happened. Picasso was no doubt talented but it was a talent that was nurtured and developed. All through his career he experimented and improved, challenged previous work to make the new better, trying new avenues and in various aspects constantly striving for improvement. It also took time for him to be established. The first decade of his career was spent developing a proper platform and it took another decade to get firmly established. All this was to build the product experience of the Picasso brand (although it was of course not expressed that way).

---

The Picasso brand was established with the help of solid product values and some inspired communication. A contemporary artist, also from Spain, provides an interesting comparison: Salvador Dali.

The examples of Picasso and Dali show that a brand has to be built on a solid product foundation, communication is important but cannot compensate for poor quality – at least in the medium to long term, and quality control is essential in order to maintain the brand perception.

---

## *Example*

Dali was at one stage almost as highly rated as Picasso, and his work commanded huge premiums on the international art market. Dali, compared to Picasso, focused much of his attention on communication, his life seemed as flamboyant and extreme as his art. Over time, though, the art of Dali was of much less dynamism, less constant development and in due course, for various reasons, the quality control was almost abandoned and it has been claimed, almost 'anything' was put in front of Dali for signature and consequently sold off. Today, Dali is almost totally out of favour and the premium price of his art has declined, especially in comparison with Picasso.

---

In the more traditional world of goods and services, the best example of branding is probably BMW, at least in Europe.

---

## *Example*

BMW has a long tradition of car and motorcycle manufacture, founded in 1928, but it has not always been a leading brand. In 1959 the company was virtually bankrupt and on the verge of being taken over by Daimler-Benz. The first step towards the current position was the launch of the 1500 model in 1962; but still in 1972 the turnover was only DM2000 million, at the time significantly smaller than for instance Volvo. During the late 1970s and early 1980s BMW established itself as a producer of cars that are enjoyable to drive, as expressed in the UK advertising 'the ultimate driving machine' and by 1996 BMW was one of the world's ten largest car manufacturers making over 1 million vehicles with around 650,000 cars under the BMW brand. Not least, this has been achieved with excellent profitability.

---

The case of BMW is excellent because it illustrates the effectiveness of: (a) a distinct positioning – the ultimate driving machine; (b) the power of a product that actually delivers on the brand promise; (c) distinct, differentiating and highly relevant advertising – with total focus on the machine and absence of traditional car advertising 'props' such as beautiful people and exotic location; and (d) a graphic identity which is consistently implemented down to the last detail as well as being in harmony with the brand personality.

For the communication to be effective, it is essential that it is linked to the product experience, and has a common heritage. Although this is an obvious point, many brands fail at least on implementation. For the communication to be seen as credible and indeed to build brand values, it has to be consistent with the positioning (see Part 3) and of course the brand experience. It is not unusual with advertising, also for supposedly well-managed brands, that it is built around 'tricks' to create attention but where these tricks are of no relevance to the brand at all.

The brand conceptualizes the reputation of the company or its products and as such the power of the brand is a consequence of what has happened in the past, or to be absolutely correct, the perception of what has happened in the past. An unfortunate incident or a slip in product quality can have long-lasting effects. In the 1950s Opel in Scandinavia experienced problems with corrosion due to some changes in the paint process. It took over ten years for the brand to get rid of this 'taint' despite having corrected the problem early on.

One branding activity not covered so far is rebranding, changing the brand name. This does not happen very often as for a well-known brand it is not only a major exercise in itself, and as such is costly, it also carries some significant risks. The reason for changing the brand differs, it can be that the original brand is no longer suitable, that as the brand has grown global the original brand is not possible to use any more, or the company decides that the brands should be globally aligned, i.e. the same brand for the same product.

Many executives with only a superficial grasp of the brand building process still believe that the main part of building a brand is striking advertising. Of course, this is not true. Excellent advertising is highly desirable, in particular to create trial; but successful and strong brands with high repeat purchase rates are built on a positive customer experience which, ideally, has been enhanced by effective communication programmes.

## *Examples*

One of the most written about brand changes was from Esso to Exxon in 1973 at a cost of, at the time, $100 million. In this case the reason was that the Esso brand, short for Standard Oil, was not totally controlled by Standard Oil New Jersey – a consequence of the break up of Standard Oil in 1911. Some of the reasons for choosing Exxon was that it was a unique expression, shared the first letter with Esso and was of approximately the same length.

## *Examples*

Another example is the rebranding of Mars' chocolate bar Marathon to Snickers in the UK. In this instance the reason was to streamline the branding on a global level. The rebranding was advertised and of course communicated on the wrapper of the bar; the consumers were informed, in stages, of the forthcoming name change. Due to the attention generated sales actually increased due to the rebranding rather than, as feared, declined. A good example of creating an advantage out of what was seen and perceived by many as a problem.

# 4
## The brand values

At the core of successful marketing lies the understanding that all brands are built out of key values. Or put differently, the customers' perceptions of strong, successful brands are made up of several different value dimensions. A soft drink brand can be seen as refreshing, trustworthy and socially acceptable to drink and a car brand can be safe, reliable and suitable for families, plus perhaps several other value dimensions. To understand which values are important to the target group and which ones are connected to a specific brand is an important dimension of successful brand management.

There are two fundamental facts to bear in mind in the context of brands' values. First, successful brands are built on a combination of product benefits, mainly tangible values, and emotion, values of abstract, or intangible, character. It is the combination that is important, a brand building programme must cover both aspects of the value spectrum as otherwise the efforts will 'limp'. It is not enough for a soft drink to be seen as youthful, trendy and fun, it also has to deliver on taste and refreshment. This applies to small everyday purchases as well as luxury items. As an illustration, review Rolex advertising. Rolex is probably the most successful luxury watch. The advertising constantly focuses on the functional benefits of the watch, not the snob appeal, which, presumably, comes as an effect of the price and thus rarity value and the people shown to wear the watch.

In addition, it is worth noting that some values are almost

totally tangible or abstract in character, others are a mix. For the sake of simplicity we will in the following refer to values as tangible or abstract but please note that the reality it is not quite so one-dimensional.

Second, for most product sectors, only a few value dimensions are of importance. It is often only three to four dimensions that have a significant impact across the customer base, and it is rarely more than six or seven. This has the advantage that a value enhancing process to boost the perception of a brand can focus on a limited number of values, which is easier to handle. The disadvantage is that if one or two value dimensions are neglected, the brand is behind even before you have started. If five value dimensions are important for the purchase of a product and then one of these is ignored, that means that only 80% – assuming that the values are of equal importance – of the brand will be enhanced and 20% ignored.

A further general issue is why we look at brands as being a combination of values, and not a singular totality. The reason is two-fold. The first one is that in order to be able to enhance the brand, one must dissect first as otherwise the process becomes unmanageable. By splitting the perception of the brand into the values that make up the totality, one can in a focused way improve each part of the value spectrum which will in turn result in a stronger brand. In this way the value enhancement programme (a necessity for offering superior perceived values) will focus on the right issues. It is not sufficient to tell manufacturing, R&D or marketing communication executives that the values of the brand need to be improved. That is obviously of limited use. What is required is a thorough analysis of the various values that make up the brand, or sub-brand, so that each value can be looked at and if appropriate enhanced, a process of dissecting to get to the dimensions of the brand that can be improved.

The second reason is that different aspects of the brand are of differing importance to various customers. By looking at these aspects, values, by themselves we ensure that the brand profile is not weakened in respect of important customer groups. But a warning, this does not mean that it is advisable to have a 'split personality'. The values as a totality make up the brand profile and it is this totality that needs to be clearly defined and distinctly positioned so that it is seen by the ultimate customer as one unit. It is as important to put the values together again as it is to correctly dissect them in the first place.

Traditionally marketing focused on only one value, the USP (Unique Selling Proposition); brands are, however, not that simplistic. To ensure that you are successful it is not enough to focus on one dimension, you have to fulfil all the basic criteria for market success as well as having some element of distinction. In marketing communication the decision might well be one of focusing only on the USP or only on one aspect of the brand personality or indeed on a single-minded positioning. This does not mean that the other aspects of the brand can be ignored. While all airlines have to ensure that they are safe and usually aspire to take-off and arrive on schedule, in communication they talk about a wide network (American Airlines) and friendly service (Singapore Airlines). No one of these companies, or any other airline, will succeed if they ignore the basic aspects of the business and they will not survive in the longer term if they do not improve these fundamental basics of the service.

## GENERAL AND BRAND-SPECIFIC VALUES

The first way of analysing and dividing up the value dimensions of a brand is to look at which values are relevant to all brands in the sector and which ones are uniquely connected to specific brands. The former are called general values and the latter brand-specific, or just specific, values.

The *general values* are those values that apply to all brands in the market sector, the key dimensions required to be considered as a real alternative to the customers, without them you do not even have the potential of getting on the shopping list, whether the list is one of potential companies for the tender of a building project or a housewife's weekly shopping. For instance, for a brand to succeed in the food market, it has to fulfil the basic criteria of taste and safety. If it does not taste good, it will not succeed; and, of course, if it is seen as unsafe, it is also unlikely to succeed. These two aspects, taste and safety, are general values in the food market.

The general values apply to all brands but of course each individual brand will deliver on these values to a varying extent. The important thing to remember is that all brands are judged on these value dimensions. The general values serve as the entry ticket to the sector. To get acceptance among the customer groups, you have to perform at least to a reasonable standard. For instance, a health food product almost regardless of the health claim will never be a great success unless the taste is on parity with normal food products.

If you want your brand to be big, it is essential to master and preferably excel in the general values. A successful film needs to be entertaining, a television set needs to deliver a sharp picture, a soft drink needs to be refreshing, etc. A small niche brand can of course survive despite poor performance of the general values but the future will always be difficult and uncertain, and it will remain in the niche.

Sometimes companies think that a very strong more specific value will outweigh a weak performance in the general values. This is rarely so. If a car is not easy to drive, all other features will not help very much. If a bank has excellent ethical credentials but has very poor service and low interest rates for savers, it will not attract the funds of the average consumers. While the general values provide the entry ticket to the sector and the minds of the customers, the *specific values* are the ones that differentiate the winners from the average. A specific value is a value that is particular to *one* brand. It is a value dimension that only one (or perhaps a few) brand has mastered and made its own.

The specific values are the ones that create a distinct profile, one that sets one brand apart from another. Preferably a specific value should be unique and inimitable so that they become value dimensions intrinsically linked to only one particular brand. Unfortunately due to ingenuity of competitors this is becoming increasingly difficult to achieve, especially in respect of tangible values.

The general values are at the foundation of the value mix. You have to be strong in general values to be a big brand, it is not necessary to excel but a perception at least on par with the main competitors is recommended. The specific values is what gives a general brand a profile, a set of unique characteristics which sets the brand apart from bland competitors, creating a distinct profile. From this follows that for a brand to be successful and gain a superior market position both general and specific values are needed.

---

# *Example*

Uncle Ben's rice from the Mars Corporation is an example of successful value enhancement. In most markets in Europe Uncle Ben's is retailed at a price premium of over 100% compared to the generic product, in some instances being up to three times as expensive as lower-priced alternatives. One part of Uncle Ben's value proposition is the non-stickiness of the rice, each grain of rice is separate. The manufacturing technique to make a non-sticky rice has meant that Uncle Ben's has a distinct profile, a specific value. Uncle Ben's has by now become almost a victim of its own success in that this value is no longer exclusively Uncle Ben's property; the value has in many countries been transferred into a general value in that all rice sold has to be non-sticky, even Chinese rice which traditionally is supposed to be sticky.

---

## TANGIBLE AND ABSTRACT VALUES

When looking at a value dimension, such as taste or trust, each value is predominantly either tangible or abstract in character. The tangible aspect of a value dimension is one which is related to 'real' aspects of the brand, how the product performs, how the service is carried out. If it is tangible, then it can be assessed objectively, it is concrete, touchable and in principle possible to assess objectively. The reliability of a car is such a value, you can objectively measure whether a car is reliable or not. The consistent quality of the hamburgers served at McDonald's is another example of such a value.

As the track record of successful brands indicates that the tangible aspects are at the core of a brand's success, a company can never spend enough time on getting these values to the best possible standard, *within the cost parameters*. There is obviously no point in adding values, if the addition to the value dimension or the creation of the value costs more than what the customers are prepared to pay for the changes. There are, though, no risks as such connected to adding tangible value dimensions of no interest to the customers, they will just be ignored. No harm done in the customer perceptions, only in that company resources have been wasted.

The abstract, intangible aspect of values is related to the emotional side of the brand. Such a value is related to the feelings we have about the brand and perhaps also the market sector. It is of course subjective, as all feelings are subjective and definitely impossible to touch.

While the tangible aspects can be expanded and elaborated upon without any negative effects, the abstract values are different – too many dimensions and the customers will be confused. If the company tries to build a complex set of abstract value dimensions, it will fail as the customers are unlikely to be able to take it all in, and while in the tangible case the customers will just ignore the additional values, in this case, the values will be communicated and as such cause confusion.

The distinct split of values into tangible and abstract ones is useful from an analytical and practical point of view as it makes it easier to focus and achieve progress. The reality is, as mentioned earlier, more complex. A tangible value is not exclusively 'hard' and a tangible value dimension is not exclusively determined by the hard facts; the intangible, communicative aspects do have an influence as well. The driving experience of a car, which might be a key value is in character tangible but the perception of the value can very well be influenced by abstract dimensions, established with the help of advertising or some other form of communication.

Similarly, an abstract value such as trust is not exclusively about emotions. If the company does not in its activities show that it is to be trusted, the hard facts will invariably influence the abstract trust value dimension.

For a simple first analysis of a brand the recommendation is to first define the key values, thinking in terms of both abstract and tangible aspects. When the key values have been defined and the enhancement process starts, a more detailed review of the main aspects of the most important value dimensions should cover both the tangible and the abstract sides of the value.

---

## *Example*

Rover cars is a brand that has been further revitalized as part of BMW. One key value dimension for Rover is 'Britishness' but to be effective further definition was required. The conclusion of much work and soul-searching was that Britishness was 'relaxed motoring', enhanced by wood panelling and the smell of real leather. A case of an abstract dimension enhanced by tangible aspects.

The focus on Rover's Britishness has the advantage from the BMW point of view in attracting in the main different customers than the BMW brand values symbolized by the ultimate driving machine.

---

### THE VALUE SPECTRUM

The value spectrum, or value mix, of a brand is made up of all the different value dimensions. A strong brand position will be achieved by correctly managing the set of values. Successful brands have strong general values coupled with one or two company-specific ones, a combination of focus and broad perspective; focus in that only a few values are singled out, broad perspective in that it is not only one dimension that is important, the brand needs to communicate several values.

BMW, one of the strongest and best managed brands in the world is, of course, a safe and reliable car, fulfilling the general values required of a family saloon. To become a strong brand it has built a very strong position as a car worthy of a 'real' driver. A strong specific value making the brand distinct and appealing.

To analyse the value spectrum of a brand a simple matrix can be useful (see Figure 4.1).

In most cases it is recommended to do the analysis in the numbered sequence. Also the sequence is usually the order in which one should look at the value enhancing process.

First one has to ensure that the basic tangible aspects are in place, if they are missing everything else will be in vain. Once that has been established it makes sense to review the tangible specific dimensions against the background of the general values, what, if any, tangible unique values does the brand represent. If not, can any be created?

|  | General | Specific |
|---|---|---|
| Tangible | 1 | 2 |
| Abstract | 3 | 4 |

**Figure 4.1**   *The value spectrum matrix*

The second phase involves the abstract aspects. Does the brand's credibility stand up to the required values? Is it trusted, familiar, safe or whatever the key dimensions are? As per the tangible aspects, it is important to correctly assess the situation to ensure that there is confidence in the market for building a more specific profile. The abstract specific values are what really can set one brand apart from another, and even perhaps form the basis of the whole positioning. If there are no specific abstract values of any strength, can a dormant value be vitalized, or can one be created from scratch? Does the company have resources for such an exercise?

From our experience of working with the value spectrum of different brands in different countries we have observed that the cultural aspects play a role in how values are built. For instance in the UK, companies are usually quick to assess the abstract values and most brands have at least a nugget of specific abstract values, and certainly effort has gone into creating these values. Traditionally, however, the specific tangible values have been neglected and even the general tangible ones have in some instances been, if not ignored, given insufficient attention. On the other hand, for instance in Scandinavia, the situation is almost the reverse. General tangible values are very well taken care of and general abstract values, at least the most obvious ones, are also well-handled. But the specific values are often ignored, in particular the specific abstract ones where very few brands have a satisfactory situation.

Two conclusions can be drawn from this. First, it appears that in a small country, or a small market, the general values become more important as, perhaps not surprisingly, there is limited competition so less need for a distinct profile, specific values. Second, if the business community is focused on production and engineering, the tangible aspects take precedent, but if the main interest lies in communication and building a distinct profile in the market place, it is the specific abstract values that draw the attention. The purpose of highlighting this is that by looking at the market place and the competition, it is possible to find ways of building values which contradict the established fashion and thus create a competitive advantage.

All through this book the focus is on the positive values and how you make them as strong as possible, perhaps with the exception of the short section on crisis management in the chapter on PR. A brand can, however, also carry negative values, such as being seen as inhuman or corrupt. If widely held, or with the risk of them being widely spread, the company must defuse or negate these dimensions, a task requiring great skill.

Finally, the value spectra are not static. The normal trend is that a specific value becomes general as competitors copy market initiatives. But the reverse is also possible, to take a general value and make it specific, hi-jacking a specific dimension of a brand value.

The reason for establishing the value spectrum of a brand, and its competitors, is to understand the strengths and weaknesses of the brand so that it becomes possible to focus development resources in the right direction, building a stronger brand for the future. The ultimate objective for all marketers in this respect is to make the values so strong that the perceived values of a brand are strong enough to make the price perceptions fade and become almost irrelevant.

---

## *Example*

Whisky is a category where the main stream brands have little distinction and where performance has been disappointing for many. At the same time, premium whiskies have shown good growth and perhaps more importantly raised the general awareness of quality in whiskies.

Taste, real and perceived, is a key general value for whisky. A factual part of the taste of a whisky is the length of time the drink has been stored. Super-premium whiskies are known as 12-year or 20-year-olds, apparently you can even buy a 60-year-old for over £3,000/bottle.

Bell's is a leading Scotch whisky brand, according to AC Nielsen the best selling alcoholic drink in the UK with take-home sales of £128.8 million in 1997. A key element of the taste perception is age, i.e. for how long the whisky has been allowed to mature. In 1994 Bell's took the general value of taste as enhanced by age and made it into a company specific value dimension by making its drink the whisky that has been aged for eight years, as opposed to six for other premium whiskies and two to four for regular whisky. The general value of taste was given a specific dimension and Bell's all of a sudden had a stronger and distinct taste value. One advantage of this strategy seems to be that it is very difficult to imitate, especially in the short term as you need to wait for an extra two years to make a 6-year-old whisky an 8-year-old one. As they said at the time of launch: 'We decided to give you an even better whisky. Eight years ago.'

# 5
# Pricing in the brand development process

Setting the right price for a product or service is an art that many marketers do not master. In my view the market trader is as a rule much more likely to get the price right than a traditionally trained marketer. The process of actually aiming for setting the best price will be covered in Part 3 of this book; at this stage we will only look at the principles of pricing and how it fits into the brand building process.

As indicated earlier, one of the objectives with building a strong brand is to reduce the importance of price, make the brand's values so strong that the customers will buy without paying too much attention to the price. This is an ideal situation, rarely happening in real life.

The price of a product or service serves as a balance to the value spectrum. The positive values of the brand build up a perception in the minds of the customers, the price then comes in as a 'cut-off' point – if the price is too high in respect of the perception of value, there will be no purchase. On the other hand, if the price is such that it is below what one would expect from such a set of values, the customer will buy. All in all, a very simple concept.

Price and brand values can be seen as a set of scales, the values on one side and price on the other (see Figure 5.1). If the values outweigh the price, the customer will buy, if not, no purchase or the competitor will get the purchase.

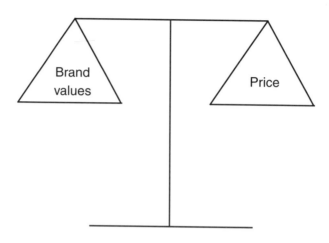

**Figure 5.1** *Brand values versus price*

The strength of brand values is a function of perceptions, how a certain dimension is perceived by the customers. While pricing on the face of it is concrete and one-dimensional, it is also a question of perception. It is not the actual price which determines the price cut-off point mentioned earlier, it is the perceived price.

In some instances, such as handling a tender or a big written quotation, the perceived price and the actual one are very close or even the same. When it comes to consumer goods and in particular smaller items, the perceived price can be different from the actual one. Very few people have a clear view of how much different items cost and as most consumer purchasing situations represent a choice between different alternatives, such as shall we have meat or fish for dinner, what kind of coffee, white or brown bread, the decision making is based on perceptions of values and perceptions of prices. Some prices are familiar to everyone, a half kilo of the brand leader's R&G coffee in many European countries is something most housewives know the price of, while not many could mention the price of a jar of horseradish.

## *Example*

A manufacturer of horseradish sauce once told me that his was the ideal product to market. Almost everyone would like to buy but they bought in such limited quantities that the price of one jar did not make much difference. But the reason for his success was not greediness, no, in this case it was also a question of product quality. The consumers did not mind paying extra but they did expect the best quality which was what he provided. He earned a very nice living!

The products where prices are familiar to the majority of customers are called KVIs, Key Value Items. These are also the items which to a large extent determine the price profile of a company, especially in retailing. As neither the customers nor the competitors can focus on all prices in a supermarket with 25,000 items, a hundred or so items are singled out and the prices are monitored with the greatest care. The price perception of a retailer is created by these 100–200 items, not the other 24,800. This said, the general price level cannot be much out of line as you will then sooner or later be found out but the same level of attention is not required.

At the launch of discount retail stores in the 1960s, the number of items were set at 600–800, no more. The reason was not based on purchasing or stock-holding principles. As the goods were not individually price marked to save money, the number of items were restricted to what a skilled cashier could remember.

The importance of understanding the difference between perceived price and actual price is one dimension of the pricing process. Another is to understand what the price actually is.

Most products have a published price but that is rarely the whole story. The official price is just the starting point. Many companies have bonus schemes which favour large purchases as a large shipment is cheaper per unit than many small ones; they have schemes favouring large customers as a large customer can be more important than a small one, and they probably have promotional programmes which would give discounts at certain times on certain products. This means that the actual, factual price can be quite difficult to assess, especially if one also takes into consideration the costs of the buyer to acquire the goods, such as extra handling costs for low cost items, and freight and insurance charges.

The purpose here is not to give a detailed description of the pricing process, just to highlight the complexity of the issue so that appropriate care is taken to ensure that: (a) the price perception is at least as favourable as the reality; (b) the price perception is competitive; (c) the customers' perception of the brand's values is not below that of the price perception; and (d) the KVIs in the sector are well-defined and handled accordingly.

# 6
# Brand terminology

Many marketing books are filled with new terms and expressions. The purpose here is not to introduce new terms, only to define and elaborate on some key concepts and in the process put a perspective in place for the chapter on the brand hierarchy, how brands in a company relate to each other.

Originally the manufacturer or service provider would just put his name on a product, in most cases without much further consideration. Once the first product was launched and successful, he/she would then think about the next one, should it carry the same name but with a different description or should it have a totally new name? The former was, for instance, the policy of H J Heinz and the latter Procter & Gamble.

## FROM CORPORATE TO PRODUCT BRANDS

Since the time of the branding pioneers the situation has become more complex and we now have several different types of brands. One set of brand concepts refers to how the product is branded in relation to name of the company. The main ones are

- corporate brands
- house brands
- range brands
- product brands.

In some companies the expressions might overlap, for instance corporate and house brand might be the same and a product brand is also a range brand.

## Corporate brand

The *corporate brand* is a brand symbol covering all activities of a corporation. It clearly and distinctly identifies the one who is responsible for the product or service. It is not so much a value symbol as a piece of information for the customers who really want to know. Its primary purpose is not to convey a distinct set of values, it is more an issue of providing information and perhaps some general overriding reassurance. The use of corporate brands have increased in recent times for mainly two reasons. First, there is an increasing interest, at least in the consumer market, for knowing who is really behind a brand and a product, usually to answer questions like 'Is this a trustworthy company?' and 'Does this company behave in the way I think it should?'. Second, the Western companies have seen how the Asian, and in particular the Japanese, companies have put much more focus on this aspect. The reason, presumably, is that the Asian market takes a different view on the role of branding, or perhaps more accurately, the issue mentioned previously is of greater importance and has been so for a longer period than in the West.

If handled properly a corporate brand will do little damage and might add a sense of confidence to some customers. To use a corporate brand as the main brand for building values is not to be recommended unless the corporate range of product is limited. The reason is that if a brand has to represent a wide range of products and services, perhaps with few common denominators, the values of the brand can only be of the general type, such as trustworthy, reliable, etc. which in most cases is not sufficient for building a strong brand. The corporate brand consequently often takes a back seat position in the brand communication.

*Example*

Almost all of Nestlé's products worldwide carry the 'nest' logo, usually at the back of the pack in a low-key position. The logo is there to serve as an ultimate guarantee and to tie the different brands together in a subtle way. The logo is, however, not on all products. Buitoni, Nestlé's Italian food brand, does not have the logo, as it would be seen as inconsistent with a positioning as the authentic Italian brand to have the Swiss parent demonstrating its ownership on the pack. The eye-care brand Alcon, another Nestlé subsidiary, is also without the corporate endorsement as it is not seen as an advantage to highlight the food and drink brand connection.

### House brand

The *house brand* is one of the most traditional ways of branding. A house brand is when one brand is used across a number of products, prime examples from the consumer goods sector are Heinz and Kellogg's but also McDonald's follows the same principle as do most banks. Notable exceptions are some consumer goods sectors such as detergents with P&G and Unilever and confectionery with brands such as KitKat and Snickers from Nestlé and Mars, but in the majority of cases, the house brand policy is followed. The house brand is usually the name of the company or the founder, such as BMW and Ford, but can also be an invented name such as Kodak.

If the product range of a house brand is too wide, the customers will either look at the brand as one with a uninteresting profile – as the house brand must be general in nature to cover all the different types of products – or the customers will develop their own sub-brands within the house brand. Some food brands are examples of the latter, such as Heinz in the UK, and to a degree in the US, and Dr Oetker in Germany. Heinz' canned soups, baked beans and ketchup are seen by many as each having a distinct brand profile, Dr Oetker's cake mixes and frozen pizzas no doubt have different brand values.

The advantage of using a house brand is that it is easy to connect the product and the company and that a house brand almost always covers several products and consequently a high turnover, which makes marketing investments relatively less expensive. The disadvantage is that the profile can easily become rather bland in that it has to cover many different products and services. For a company with a fairly homogeneous product portfolio, such as BMW and McDonald's mentioned earlier, the house brand strategy is sensible, if the product range is much wider the 'blandness' factor might be too important to allow effective use of a house brand.

### Range based

The next level of brands is represented by the *range brand*, sometimes also called product group brand. This is a brand used for a number of products or services and this set has a number of common, distinct values. The range brand can either be freestanding, such as Fairy detergents (called Yes in some European markets) from P&G, or Lynx personal care products from Unilever, or they can be a sub-brand to a house brand such as the BMW 5-series or Ford Mondeo.

The range brands have often been created with the explicit intention of having a unifying symbol for a range of products. With the help of the brand, a range of products can be presented as a unity with a set of common characteristics. It is a symbol which credibly can be communicated and it is possible to make this communication, in whatever form it takes, distinct and attractive.

It is this commonality in combination with a reasonable sales volume which makes the concept of a range brand so interesting and useful. The disadvantage is that the method requires self-discipline to avoid loading too many different products under the same umbrella. If that is done, the profile becomes diluted, communication becomes less effective and, if the worst comes to the worst, the original products might lose some of their attractiveness.

The importance of range brands has increased in recent years for two reasons. First, in the more developed brand building companies, many product brands have been transformed into range brands to get greater sales volumes and exploit the position of the product brand. The above-mentioned Fairy is one example. Originally the brand was only used on washing-up liquid but has now been extended to detergents and washing machine powder. Another example is the Mars bar, originally only in the one bar form and one taste but now available – depending on the country – in for instance different flavours of chocolate and in different sizes from bite size in cartons to king size bars. An extension into a light version appears, however, to have run into problems in the UK, perhaps not surprisingly as the traditional bar was closely linked to an energy boosting value dimension which is the opposite to 'light'. However, the Mars bar has been successfully added to the ice cream sector.

Second, the range brand has become a way of grouping a product range into manageable units. This has happened in many companies without a long tradition of brand management and the range brand has provided a vehicle for creating brand concepts which can be clearly communicated.

*Example*

This was the strategy we helped to create and implement for a European ice cream company. Traditionally so called street sales of ice cream, i.e. individually wrapped items, is based on a wide range of products, from a cheap lolly type ice cream to an elaborate ice cream cone, in total perhaps twenty items. As each outlet usually only carries one brand, the brand in question must provide a full range while at the same time there is little point in having too many items as the kiosk or corner shop will only have a small freezer.

In this particular case the policy of the company had been to have a strong house brand and then individual names for each item which meant that nowhere was there sufficient volume for building a distinct identity for anything but the house brand. Most importantly, the main part of the range, ice cream cones, were only called ice cream cones followed by the flavour. This had been acceptable (just about) in the past but the company faced a serious threat in that the market was about to be attacked by a strong foreign company.

Having identified the threat, we created 150 different range brand alternatives which through a two-stage screening process and a market research programme resulted in a new range brand for the ice cream cones with a distinct and positive identity. The new range brand became the focus of attention, new packaging and advertising was developed consistent with the positioning and brand values, and the commercial end result was that sales increased by around 20%, and this from a brand leading position and, perhaps as important, the competitive attack was not successful.

## Product brand

The most specific form of branding is to apply the product branding strategy, i.e. one product – one brand. The advantages and disadvantages are obvious. The advantage is that you can be very focused, the disadvantage is one of scale – the turnover and amount of product to carry the brand investment might be limited. This is, though, how many brands start out. The first Mars bar, the first Ivory soap, the first Ford (although called model T there was only one model and one colour), the original Coca-Cola, etc.

The product brand can, as the range brand, either be freestanding with no apparent link to any other brand symbol, or be a separate brand but under the umbrella of a range or house brand. There are very few pure free-standing single product brands left in the traditional branded goods markets. Most of them have been converted into range brands or at least extensions have been tried. Not even Guinness, the famous black stout, has been exempt. Campari is one of the few that has remained focused on its one product, combining in one both product and house brand.

It is more common to have a product brand that is linked to a range or house brand, although in many cases the product brand is soon transformed into a range brand. The original Magnum ice cream was a one product brand under the Unilever house brand of the market in question (such as Wall's, Lagnese or Algida) but it has since been extended. Other examples are Diet Coke as a product brand in the Coca-Cola family and Intel Pentium as one of several product brands of Intel.

The terminology in itself is of course only of interest as a way of understanding what people mean. But a review of the various opportunities will also provide a framework for the various possibilities of branding a product or service, a decision which should be taken with the greatest care as it will influence the potential for creating a distinct brand.

## BRAND EXPRESSIONS DEPENDING ON MARKET POSITION

The above section is mainly about brand concepts in relation to identifying a suitable brand for a product or product range within a company. The following will bring in terms to identify how a brand is perceived and positioned in relation to competitive brands in the market sector. There are three main expressions in this context:

- primary brand
- secondary brand
- tertiary brand.

Admittedly not a very imaginative set of expressions but adequate and generally accepted.

### Primary brand

A *primary* brand is a brand leader, in other words a brand that is strong in the market place and is generally regarded as a 'benchmark' brand. In principle each market sector will have only one primary brand but there are exceptions, for instance if two brands share the market leadership, such as Unilever and P&G in detergents with brands such as Persil/Omo and Ariel respectively.

A primary brand will have a high awareness and be generally well-known among the customers. In case of FMCG it will be a 'must stock' item for retailers, in other markets it will be an obvious choice, one that a buyer can choose without taking any risks.

## Secondary brand

A *secondary* brand is positioned as number two, three or four in a market sector. It will have a good reputation but is a brand that a customer would choose more as a result of nothing else being available than as a pro-active choice. Traditionally, secondary brands have survived on the basis of distribution strengths, i.e. being available rather than being chosen. The product is often a me-too of the brand leader. A consequence of the market position is that the brand is often sold on a price platform, forced to cut prices in order to sell as the brand often lacks any distinct brand values. (If it had any, it would not be a secondary but probably a primary brand.)

Many secondary brands have disappeared as the raison d'être for a secondary brand is usually to give a distributor or a customer a tool with which to keep the brand leader from abusing its position of strength. That tactic is in most markets no longer necessary. Also in market sectors with high demands on distribution efficiency they have disappeared as there is just not room for the brand any more. A UK example of a secondary brand was Crosse & Blackwell canned soups and baked beans, in both cases third or fourth to Heinz and retailers' own label. Consequently Crosse & Blackwell has now disappeared from the canned market. In the car industry in the US Chrysler has on and off been in the secondary brand position and certainly American Motors in its day was a typical secondary brand. Today some car brands of Asian origin are in this situation.

## Tertiary based

*Tertiary* brands is a concept that is more unusual and not present in all markets. A tertiary brand is selling at a heavy discount to the brand leader, say 25–30%, it is of average quality and usually without much of a brand profile, apart from being cheap. The difference between a secondary and tertiary brand is that the latter is designed from the start to be 'cheap and cheerful' while the secondary brand aspires to be treated with the same respect as a primary brand. Tertiary brands are often 'traded', have a short-term approach and come from factories with either a distinct cost advantage or low profit expectations.

Some brands manage to move away from being a tertiary brand. For instance some of the Japanese products coming over to Europe and the US in the 1950s were seen as tertiary brands but over time they have moved up the ladder and are now in many instances the primary brands. But it took several decades of hard work.

These three expressions, primary, secondary and tertiary brands, are useful as a way classifying the position of the company's brands. A primary brand is worthy of considerable care and attention to maintain the position, secondary brands face a very uncertain future and if the company has many secondary brands it is in a very dangerous position; and finally, if a company is focusing on tertiary brands, well, this book is of little relevance as most tertiary brands are not real brands, and unlikely to become so, they are just products with a name.

## SOME OTHER EXPRESSIONS

In addition to the two types of classifications above, there are some other expression well worth being aware of and fully understanding, in particular in respect of consumer goods.

The main part of brands in the consumer goods market are manufacturers' brands. Examples are Heinz, Volkswagen, Electrolux, l'Oréal and Compaq.

### Channel brand

But there are other ways of running a brand policy. One is to use channel brands, i.e. a specific brand for each main distribution channel. This is a strategy used, for instance, in electrical household products where a company might use one brand for discount stores and another for the more upmarket retailers. Electrolux applied it for a number of years by selling Electrolux 'white' goods through one distribution channel and Husqvarna through another, the products themselves being very similar.

Channel brands seem to be declining in importance as it goes against the need for getting economies in brand building and it can also be seen by alert consumers as an attempt to hide the reality behind a brand screen.

### Own label

A more popular concept is retailer or distributor's *own labels* (O/L) or own brands. This is also called private label (P/L) or distributor's own label (DOB). Virtually all leading consumer goods retailers have an own label and own label account for almost two-thirds of all goods sold in leading UK retailers such as Tesco and Sainsbury's. The own label share is close to 100% in Marks & Spencer as well as in IKEA, the world's largest home furnishing retailer.

The difference between a channel brand and an own label is that the former is controlled by the manufacturers and is sold through several different retailers or distributors while the latter is controlled by the retailer and produced on a co-packing basis by contracted manufacturers. From a brand building perspective there is no difference, the same principles apply which is why the phenomenon of own label as such is not dealt with in any further detail.

### Co-branding

*Co-branding* is a technique that has been in use for a long time but during the 1990s has become more popular. There are two types of co-branding, first where two brands jointly endorse the product, and second where one brand endorses the contents, or part of the contents, of the main brand. A classical example in using the first approach in communication is American Express advertising featuring famous hotels and restaurants taking the American Express card.

On a product level many credit cards have dual branding, such as NatWest Visa card. Assuming that the brands are compatible this form of co-branding can be an effective way of building both brands.

The second co-branding approach is less extensively used but some companies have achieved considerable success by taking the endorsement route. The host-brand gets the benefit of the endorsement of a well-known supplier and both brands benefit by the co-branded product having greater perceived value. The most well-known, and probably the most successful one, is represented by Intel and 'Intel Inside' for PC processors. Other examples are Nutrasweet for soft drinks and Café de Colombia for coffee.

---

## *Example*

Colombia is the world's leading exporter of quality green coffee and the task to build and promote Café de Colombia, Colombia's coffee brand, is in the hands of the Colombian Coffee Federation (FNC), an organization controlled by and representing Colombia's over 400,000 independent coffee farmers.

The logo of Café de Colombia, featuring a coffee farmer (Juan Valdez) and his mule, is in the United States a very well-recognized symbol and in Europe increasingly so due to an extensive marketing programme including advertising and sponsorship. The FNC grants the usage of the logo as an endorsement to coffee roasters marketing a 100% Colombian coffee, i.e. a coffee that is totally made from Colombian coffee beans. The Café de Colombia logo is not the brand of the coffee, it is an endorsement supporting the roaster's own brand of coffee.

By featuring the logo the consumers are assured that the coffee is 100% Colombian and the roaster gets the benefit of being associated with an advertised and highly recognized brand.

The FNC programme works, contrary to many other 'country of origin' logos, not only because it is professionally implemented and has high recognition, but also because the product, the green coffee, is of a very high and consistent standard so that Café de Colombia is not only an origin, it represents a distinct product.

---

### Fighting brand

Finally, *fighting brands*. A fighting brand is a concept all brand managements have to be aware of, whether using it or not. This is a brand that is sold at a significant discount to the market leader, at least 20% but more likely over 30+%. It has no marketing support at all but is meant to sell on the price platform alone. It has a different formula to the main brand, a difference which is highlighted in the product information on the pack or in brochures and it is temporary. A fighting brand is introduced in order to protect the main brand when attacked by low-priced alternatives. By introducing the fighting brand, the company can maintain the primary brand's price position and use the fighting brand to claw back sales from the price-orientated competitor and then, when the mission has been accomplished and the price cutting competitor has disappeared, the fighting brand disappears as well.

The fighting brand approach, if well managed, can be very effective but it is a difficult strategy to control, and corporate pressure can make it difficult to launch and withdraw from the market as quickly as required. It is also not possible to achieve the necessary price advantages in all markets. In consumer goods most attempts in the food sector have failed, while in detergents and similar products there are examples of success.

The fighting brand is similar to a tertiary brand in the sense that it is marketed on a price platform. But the difference is that a tertiary brand is in the market to stay and needs to earn money from its low price position, while a fighting brand is temporary and can be a loss maker as the purpose is to protect the, hopefully, profitable market leader.

All the different brand concepts mentioned above, and please note that the list is not exhaustive, are tools to understand the market place better, to better evaluate what type of brands the company has and in particular what kind of brand strategy to pursue. Each brand requires a specific strategy so it is impossible to state that one approach is better than another. The only specific suggestion is that it is advisable to consider all the different concepts so that the decision taken will be against a thorough evaluation of available alternatives.

# 7
# The brand hierarchy

The brand hierarchy of a company is a tool to better understand, plan and implement brand strategies. It is a way to establish how the different brands within a company, and in particular within the realms of a house brand, relate to each other and the house brand. The hierarchy is described graphically in Figure 7.1.

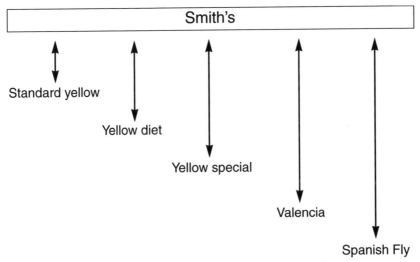

**Figure 7.1** *The brand hierarchy for a fictitious orange soft drink brand*

1. In this example Smith's is the house brand, and also the name of the company. The original product is called 'Yellow' and is

closely identified with the house brand which is why it is the closest to the house brand box.

2. The Yellow diet product is a variant of the standard. As it is a more recent product with a more up-to-date profile it is slightly more removed from the house brand than standard.

3. The Yellow Special is a line extension to the standard product. It has a different target audience but still retains some close connections to the house brand and the other 'yellow' products.

4. Finally two products with different sub-brands. Valencia has a much lower degree of Smith's branding, the label design is different from the others and has over time been given dedicated marketing support. Spanish Fly is a new product, mixing orange with alcohol and as such is differentiated away from Smith's.

The brand hierarchy can help in defining the relationship between the different brands; bring up issues such as which brands should carry the responsibility to promote the house brand; would it make sense to bring all Yellow products in the example above to the same level in relation to the house brand; should Spanish Fly be totally disconnected from Smith's, etc. Synergies can be found and weaknesses and strengths in how each product or range brand is positioned can be highlighted.

To define the synergies can have crucial impact on the cost-effectiveness of the marketing investments. As mentioned earlier economies of scale are very important in building brands as if a brand is successfully covering four instead of two products, the cost is the same. However, if the addition of products leads to a less distinct brand, the accountancy benefits will be seriously dented by a less strong brand which can ultimately damage total sales and profits.

From the perspective of the house brand it is essential that the hierarchy is correctly defined for at least one important reason and that is that a house brand's value dimensions are created by the sub-brands or products carrying the house brand. In the example above (Figure 7.1) the brand profile of Smith's is a function of all the products in the hierarchy but mostly the 'Yellow' ones as they are closest to Smith's.

Brands are in the main built from the bottom up, i.e. the products, or services, which the customers are in contact with, are the ones creating the brand profile. Even if Smith's was advertised as just Smith's Orange drinks, the main provider of brand values would still be the products as they are a much more important power in building the brand than the advertising. If the brand management of Smith's does not understand from where the brand profile is built, marketing investments can be misdirected, product brands mishandled, etc.

The brand hierarchy is one tool to understand better the relationships between brands sharing the same house brand or corporate brand. It can also be used for better structure product brands within a range brand. With the help of the hierarchy, brand management can, for instance, better define where synergies can be found and which sub-brands should perhaps be further distanced from the house brand.

# 8
# Brand stretching

Brand stretching is a term that became fashionable during the 1980s; however, as an activity it is almost as old as branding and it is still a concern for many brand managements, and will no doubt remain so for the foreseeable future. With brand stretching we mean the usage of a brand in new product or service area. For instance, taking P&G's detergents brand Ariel and using it on a washing-up liquid.

The brand hierarchy describes the usage of a brand across the company's products. It also provides an outline for assessing whether a brand can be further stretched or not. As described in the chapter on different brand expressions, there are nowadays few developed brands that are not stretched not all, i.e. only used on one singular product. In most instances attempts have been made to extend the brand.

The appeal in stretching the brand lies in the economies of scale. If the brand can be used across more products, communication investments will be lower per sales unit and ideally one product will promote the other with the same brand. To correctly assess whether a brand can take a 'stretching' or not is very difficult, one has to rely on a combination of market research, experience and common sense, realizing that none of the three on their own is likely to provide a totally reliable answer.

As indicated previously the key issue is one of compatibility of the values of the brand versus the reality of the product. Obviously the closer the two sets are to each other the easier the process. If a brand is well-established in financial services, such as a bank, it is likely that most financial products can fit this one brand, especially with the help of sub-branding. At the opposite end of the scale it is unlikely that there will be any benefits in taking the same financial services brand and putting it on a food product or a machine for making micro-processors.

One other aspect to bear in mind is that the higher up in the brand hierarchy the brand is located, the more likely it is that it will fit, but also the less distinct the values will be. A corporate brand has much greater immediate stretchability than a product brand. Nestlé as a brand stretches further than After Eight, the confectionery brand owned by Nestlé.

There is also a cultural difference. It appears that corporate brand stretching is much more common in Japan and the rest of Asia than in Europe and North America, as in Asia greater emphasis is put on the actual corporation behind the product than in the West. It seems also that brand stretching is a more effective method in smaller countries than in bigger ones, presumably due to economies of scale. A dominating house brand is more common in the smaller Scandinavian countries than in the UK and US.

An example of a corporate brand is Mitsubishi which as a brand covers a great number of activities, and Yamaha which is used as a brand on such diverse products as motorcycles and pianos.

---

## *Example*

It is not only in Asia the technique is being used. The British entrepreneur Richard Branson's 'Virgin' brand is used, in addition to the original music business and the airline Virgin Atlantic, on products and services such as cola-drinks, financial services, trains, vodka and bridal dresses. While the brand appears to be a successful carrier of values for the airline and the financial services, success has been much harder to find in the cola-business, and the Virgin vodka was in early 1998 forced out of the main part of the UK retail business. The Virgin brand is, as with Japanese examples, a symbol for Richard Branson's business interests, i.e. the 'corporate values' and as such probably closely linked to the public's perception of the man himself.

One of the more successful cases of generating revenues from a brand and at the same time building it, is Manchester United, a leading UK football club. While in North America sports clubs have long been big business and successful businesses in not only generating television coverage and getting the crowds to the stadia but also in selling branded merchandise; most clubs in Europe have been much less skilled in this respect.

---

## *Example*

At the core of the Manchester United brand is the football club. For most clubs the main purpose is to have a successful team which will draw crowds to the stadium. Manchester United has a different approach. The key is still the football team as without a winning team the rest will not work. Getting the public to the stadium is though a relatively minor revenue generator (around 20%), illustrated by the fact that it is cheaper to attend a game at Manchester United's Old Trafford stadium than at most other premier league stadia. The fans at Old Trafford appear to be more of a brand support than source of revenue, providing brand credibility by demonstrating a large local following.

The real key to the brand's success is merchandise, broadcasting rights and sponsorships. You can buy 'everything' a football fan could possibly want with the colours of Manchester United. Of course football kits and cups and hats but also, for instance, bed linen, wall paper and cakes. Manchester United even has its own television channel and, of course, a fan magazine. In the latter case it is claimed that the largest readership is in Asia.

Manchester United has managed to extend the brand to cover a great number of different products and services, it has extended the geographical base of the brand so that over 90% of the fans live outside the Manchester area and the club is very profitable with a last reported profit margin of 32% on a turnover close to £100 million. In one 6-month period the club made 'more in profits than all but four other English clubs each generated in revenues' (source *Financial Times*).

---

Brand stretching does however not always follow expectations. Kellogg's with impeccable credentials as a breakfast product brand has had considerable difficulties in moving outside of the traditional cereals market. Attempts to launch orange juice and various other breakfast products have in most instances failed in Europe (despite some success in the US).

---

## *Example*

Sears Roebuck & Co in the US is an example of both brand stretching gone too far and how to regain the focus. Sears has its origins in the 1880s and started out as a mail order company, moving into retailing in the mid-1920s. The business was built on carrying a wide range and rigorous quality control, which made Sears one of the most trusted brands and also at one stage the world's largest retailer. Sears management diversified into financial services, real estate broking (estate agencies), insurance, shopping centres and even stock-broking. In all instances with the objective to utilize people's trust in the Sears brand. While the diversification was successful in the shorter term, in the end with an increasingly competitive retail scene, the diversification led to lack of focus on the core retail business, the activity that actually provided the confidence behind the brand.

To regain credibility, and profitability, all but the retail operation was closed or sold, even including the mail order service and any stores without profit potential. With a much more focused operation and a brand that had its credibility restored, Sears went from a loss of $3 billion to a profit of $1.25 billion.

---

## *Example*

An elaborate scheme for brand stretching has been established in Asia by British American Tobacco (BAT). BAT is putting its leading brand Benson & Hedges on a range of coffee products and even a coffee shop, the Benson & Hedges Bistro. Other similar projects from BAT are Lucky Strike clothing, John Player Special Whisky and Kent Travel, a travel agency. Although the advertising possibility no doubt is of importance, the company has stated that the purpose is to make money, i.e. to ensure that the branded products and services actually provide net profit. The strategy, presumably, is to combine the long-term objective of finding growth opportunities outside the tobacco industry – which is declining in the West – with leveraging the extremely well-established brands into new sectors with the added benefit of being able to promote the brand despite various restrictions.

Brand stretching can also be used as a defensive tool to protect the company's ability to communicate and widen its appeal. Several tobacco companies have applied this strategy, such as Camel boots and Marlboro jackets and sweaters.

# 9
# International brand strategies

Although in theory there is little difference between an international or national brand strategy, they should both aim for building the strongest possible brand through enhancing the key value dimensions. In reality there are some specific issues to bear in mind when developing an international strategy, not least from a practical standpoint.

Reviewing a variety of examples one can conclude that most will fall into one of four categories:

1. A uniform, international brand profile which essentially is imposed on each country.

2. A dual strategy where the international strategy is fairly uniform but different from the home market.

3. A common framework across the world but with significant local adaptation.

4. An opportunistic approach where each decision regarding a country and market is taken in order to get the best short-term results.

The first strategy is not a very common one but has been successfully applied, more or less stringently, by several brands and companies, such as Coca-Cola and Marlboro.

The first element that has to be in place for this strategy to work is that it has to be very well-defined, with considerable practical experience in implementation. This is in order to get credibility with the staff in various countries, but also to ensure that no serious mistakes are made. It certainly seems a more appropriate strategy for a big brand than a small one, and it most probably also helps to have a big home market so that resources can be generated to fund head office development of the best strategy. While several large companies have succeeded, more than a few mid-sized US-based companies have failed in their European marketing as they have not sufficiently understood the need for local adaptation, and have not had the resources, or the brand profile, to develop a successful version of this strategy.

It also appears from observing the companies that have been successful in following this strategy, that if the brand profile is closely linked to the real or imagined life style of the home country of the brand, it is easier to implement and there are more reasons to follow it. Coca-Cola is still closely related to the American way of life and the Marlboro cowboy has a well-defined origin, although probably more related to the movies than reality.

---

## Example

Benetton as a retail brand has been successful in some instances but less so on other occasions. While the original theme of 'United colours of Benetton' almost by definition has been accepted across different markets, some other marketing initiatives have been less successful as they have run up against local opposition, being perceived as 'tasteless' and 'offensive'.

---

Other market sectors where the strategy seems to work are the ones where great commonality exists across borders among the customers, including such sectors as high-tech electronics and the higher end of the fashion and art market.

The second alternative, the dual strategy, is common among companies with a strong home market but a more careful approach to international branding. The duality lies in the fact that although the visual identity is identical and the core brand values are the same, the implementation and which dimensions to put emphasis on differ between the domestic market and the international ones.

*Example*

Volvo is the brand leader in Sweden with a share of 25–30% of the car market but outside Scandinavia, Volvo is a niche brand with a share rarely more than 1 or 2%. The brand strategy is in the one case one of mass marketing, the other one is much more focused. The core values are the same but the emphasis in the message mix is different and it is, of course, also necessary with a different product mix. In Sweden the Volvo organization requires a wide range which has led it to sell Renault's smaller models as there is no small Volvo to cover that part of the range for the dealers, while in most other countries the emphasis is almost exclusively on the large models.

The difference lies more in the implementation and where to put the emphasis than in the brand values as such. In the case of Volvo the key values have included family driving and safety plus by the mid-1990s emphasis on the driving experience. The duality is seen in that different markets focus on different aspects where, for instance, it appears that the driving experience has been given more emphasis in some markets than in others.

The dual strategy can seem schizophrenic, and it is to a degree, but in reality it is a very popular and in many cases successful international brand strategy. It combines a reasonable level of discipline with a pragmatic approach to each individual market.

The third strategy, adaptation within a framework, is most suitable for a brand aiming to establish itself in categories with a strong local tradition. The strategy is similar to the dual one but with a stronger will to adapt to local circumstances.

For the strategy to be relevant, the type of product must differ from country to country. One such market is coffee. Although the habit of drinking coffee is virtually universal, the way coffee is drunk and the taste preferences differ significantly from country to country, and even from region to region within a country. It is also a market sector where people are proud of the regional or national differences. Italians prefer Italian coffee; the Austrian thinks Austrian coffee is the best; Scandinavians consider the coffee they drink is prepared in the best possible way, etc. The coffee brands are also mainly national in their perspective, perhaps with the exception of instant coffees, and although companies such as Philip Morris/Kraft-Jacobs-Suchard are present in most European markets with brands such as Jacobs, Jacque Vabre and Gevalia, from the consumer perspective the brands are local.

To succeed in such a market it is advisable to play along with these perceptions. It is unlikely that the consumers will boost their esteem of a brand by getting to know that it is no longer a national brand but part of a big multinational. It is far more productive to adapt the strategy and position the brand as the local brand it is perceived to be. The framework can in such an instance be rather loose and basically only refer to an exchange of best practice across borders (this appears to be the strategy of Philip Morris/Jacobs), or it can be more strict where the different brands over many years are gradually moved to reflect at least partly a similar set of brand values.

The final alternative is to take a totally opportunistic approach. This might sound foolish but can be successful at least if the management in charge is aware of the product or service's intrinsic values and does not abuse them in the process of local adaptation. An opportunistic approach is in a sense what the classical marketing approach suggests, total adaptation to the local market circumstances. The disadvantages are perhaps obvious, no synergies in brand building know-how, no synergies in the creation and production of communication and conflicting messages if international media are used.

## Example

One such example is the use of the brand name Findus in Europe. Findus is Nestlé's frozen food brand in most countries outside North America but with one important exception, Italy, where the brand is controlled and used by Unilever, Nestlé's arch rival. The reason for this goes back to a series of joint ventures in the 1960s when effective control over the Findus brand in Italy went from Nestlé to Unilever. At the time, the management of Nestlé did not mind at all that the Findus brand was used in Italy, rather the reverse. They saw it as an advantage that the brand was widely spread in Europe. While the opportunism was a good strategy in the 1960s, it is unlikely to be seen as such today with the free movement of goods within the European Union.

The opportunistic strategy, although it has some short-term advantages, cannot be recommended unless specific circumstances require such an approach. It makes much more sense to use one of the other strategies so that economies of scale in the brand development process can be utilized. It is, however, recommended to bear in mind an element of opportunism in entering a market as a brand position is only worthwhile to develop if it is likely to be successful. Without short-term success, there will not be an opportunity for long-term success.

It is apparent from the above that there is not one ideal strategy for everyone even though it is more likely that the two middle strategies will be appropriate than the first one or the last one.

# 10

## Managing the brand development process

In many, if not most, cases of brand development the difference between a strong brand and failure is proper implementation. Although it is essential to get the thinking and strategy right, if the implementation is not carried out in the best possible way, the brand will fail or at least fail to reach its potential. This chapter will not cover all aspects of how to manage brand development, it is far too wide a subject to fit into one chapter. Instead we will focus on some particularly relevant issues, sometimes forgotten or ignored.

### THE GOLDEN RULES

The following four rules of brand development have been taken from an article by the former Director General of the UK Marketing Society, Mr Gordon Medcalf.

- The first brand gets the best position.
- Branding is a slow process – have patience but strike while the iron is hot.
- Don't tamper with the brand, be consistent.

- Don't waste time on losers, go for quality.

These rules are of course no more rules than any other marketing rules, they are usually applicable but not always. They do, however, focus on some important aspects of marketing and are, in my view, well worth noting.

## First brand gets the best position

The first rule, that the first brand gets the best position, is probably the most widely accepted but also the one most likely to be misinterpreted. It is not true that the first brand in a market always gets the best position. What is true is that the first brand to successfully establish itself in a market sector has a distinct head start. It was, as an example, not the first maker of video recorders that clinched that market. The first brand was Ampex but it was the VHS system that finally became the winner and with it several Japanese brands like JVC.

What the first rule says indirectly is that it is very difficult to topple a brand that is well entrenched as the brand leader. If your brand is in the market and has gained a strong position, it takes either an exceptional effort by a competitor to change this and/or the brand leader makes mistakes and thus opens the door for a challenger to succeed. The conclusion of the first rule is that ensure that your brand is first into the main position and if you are a brand leader, ensure that you stay in the first position.

## Branding is a slow process

The second rule is a combination of a plea for patience and a sense of urgency. In most cases it takes time to build a brand. Most leading brands are at least 20 years old, many are 100 years or more such as Coca-Cola, Ford and Cadbury. There are exceptions but even the Microsoft and Intel brands are over 20 years old, although actively managed as brands they are more recent.

Unless some exceptional circumstances or break-throughs take place, the branding process takes time because it takes time to establish a brand's position in the minds of a wide range of customers. If the brand is a sub-brand to a well-known house brand the process can be much quicker. When I was involved in the launch of Findus Lean Cuisine low calorie frozen meals in the mid-1980s (voted brand of the year in 1986), the brand was established within six months, both from an awareness point of view and in getting the key values across. The launch was no doubt helped by the awareness of the house brand, some effective advertising and product merchandising coupled with 'being in the right place at the right time'.

This last point is an illustration of the second part of the second rule, strike while the iron is hot. In other words, take advantage of situations to establish brand values, be opportunistic.

### Don't tamper with the brand

The third rule is the most obvious one and the one which in reality is most difficult to follow. Consistency is an important element of successful brand building. It is obvious that a brand with a consistent profile is much more trusted than one which is changing all the time. This is no different from personal relationships. Most people do not like their friends to constantly change personality, you like them because of the way they are. You like to keep them that way, or more correctly, to develop with you over time but you do not want them to flutter from one personality to another. Still that is what many brand managers do, changing the brand personality, to the detriment of the long-term future of the brand.

### Don't waste time on the losers

The final point goes back to the original reason for branding, a mark of quality. A branding process will only succeed with quality products. Quality is a subjective concept so the advice is that if a branded product or service does not generate business, there is no acceptance of the proposition of the brand, do not waste time on 'pushing water uphill', you are unlikely to succeed. It is better to spend the resources on winners.

To manage this fourth point, it is advisable to have monitoring systems in place, in particular when it comes to new brands so that brand management can follow the progress and read those initial signals from the market which is likely to indicate whether the brand will be a success or not.

## THE ACTION RULES

There are many action rules in brand development, one is to ensure that there *is* some action and not only analysis and reports. The following two rules have their origins in Procter & Gamble and are particularly relevant to the launch of a new brand:

- Win in the 'white box'.

- Then . . . support like crazy.

The first one requires some explanation. The expression 'white box' refers to blind testing. What the rule says is that the product, or indeed the service, must be of such a quality that it will win against competition in a blind test, i.e. a test without any brand shown or any marketing support of any kind.

Once the first rule has been fulfilled, the second follows. In other words it is not worthwhile to spend marketing resources, or any other company resources for that matter, unless the product marketed is superior to what is already available on the market. When that is the case, in order to become Number 1 in the sector, you have to invest in marketing support. The more you support, within reason, the more likely it is that you will succeed.

It is of course not all market sectors where it makes sense to spend vast amounts of money, and the objective with highlighting these two rules is not to encourage all companies to boost the marketing budget. The objective is to focus on the necessity of having the fundamentals in place prior to going into the market and trying to convert customers and, when doing that, giving the brand the best possible support.

## THE SEQUENCE

The brand development process is a combination of a systematic and analytical approach and often tumultuous creativity. A too rigid structure can become a strait-jacket but unless the main steps are taken in the right order, a lot of energy will be wasted. This said, the advice is to keep a note of all interesting suggestions as they come up during the process as creativity does not always follow the structure.

The branding process is a bit like travelling, you set a target, you develop a view of how to get there and as you set off the trip does not come out exactly as you had planned but you do get there in the end.

To use this analogy, you have to know where you are before you can plan your trip. The first step in the sequence is to define the state of the brand. The definition will depend on the circumstances but regardless of the status of the brand, it is essential to first define the brand situation and its environment.

For an existing brand the starting point can be either the positioning process and with it a market analysis or a brand hierarchy analysis. Defining the hierarchy and the brand position (including competitiveness, the key values, current positioning and personality) is the starting point as an enhancement process without knowing the starting point will be a waste of time. Once the situation is clarified, the enhancement process can start. Improving the key values, defining the desired positioning (see Part 3) and the brand personality, etc. This will include developing the key values to greater strength, attacking weaknesses and building on strengths.

The third step is to communicate the brand (see Figure 10.1). Developing sales arguments, advertising, PR, etc. Again there is little use in starting a communication process unless the values have been defined and the enhancement process is in place.

Although few companies will admit it, and even fewer advertising agencies, our experience is that many advertising campaigns are based on a loosely generated 'creative idea'. The market place has not been defined by the agency or the company and no effort has been made to define key values or to position the brand, let alone define the brand personality. Consequently the advertising budget is sub-optimized and the company will be wasting money. Most leading advertising agency creative directors would agree that at the core of a successful campaign lies a distinct and well-founded brief.

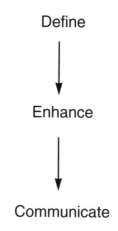

**Define**

**Enhance**

**Communicate**

**Figure 10.1**   *The brand development sequence*

It is however not enough to plan and implement the process, there needs to be control and approval systems in place.

Brand management is a concern, or should be a concern of top management. The reputation of the company's products is after all something that is of relevance to everyone in a company.

It is suggested for the management process that for each brand the company defines who is the *Brand Guardian* and who is the *Brand Developer* of the brand. The brand guardian has the ultimate responsibility for the brand and should, of course, be a senior director. The brand developer is the one driving the brand forward, developing suggestions for moving ahead. This function can be held by a marketing manager or even a brand manager. By defining who is responsible for what, one set of conflicts is avoided, namely those relating to responsibilities, and another is fostered, the one between the developer pushing things forward and the guardian keeping an eye on the longer term, consistency and ensuring that all initiatives stay within the brand's parameters. While the former type of conflicts can be destructive, the latter type will be beneficial. Already, the legendary Alfred Sloan, once CEO of General Motors, recognized that an element of conflict improves a company's performance.

The rules and management suggestions in this chapter should be seen as advice and suggestions, there are exceptions but what is stated above represents one part of brand development best practice. Hopefully it can provide at least an inspiration towards more competitive brands.

## SUMMARY OF PART 2

1. Branding is an ancient tool for identifying quality goods and services by establishing and communicating the reputation of the supplier. In today's environment it is a crucial part of a company's commercial strategy.

2. A brand is created by a combination of experience and communication, resulting in the brand being a symbol carrying a set of tangible and abstract values.

3. For a brand to succeed it first needs to fulfil the general criteria of the market as well as have a specific value profile to set it apart from competition. Second, for competitive branding, the brand needs to be seen as superior to other brands.

4. In the branding process, by correctly defining each brand's position, internally and externally, management can exploit synergies in the brand hierarchy and opportunities for successful brand.

# Part 3
## Making the brand competitive

# INTRODUCTION

Transforming brand development theory into actual strong and competitive brands is the role of brand management. Plans and a thorough understanding of how brands are built are only of use if they can be turned into action.

In this part of the book we will review some important techniques of getting the basics right, laying the foundations to the brand building, but in particular show how the brand's values can be enhanced through cost-effective use of the marketing mix. Some aspects will be covered in greater detail than others as there are limits to what can be fitted into one book, but an attempt has been made to ensure that at least most of the main aspects of the marketing mix, from the perspective of building a competitive brand, are covered.

The order of the various marketing mix dimensions is not in order of priority, apart from product development which is being dealt with first as it is, in my view, the most important part of the marketing mix in order to build a strong brand.

# 1
## Getting the foundation right

To build a proper house, you have to ensure that you have a solid foundation and that the foundation is being put down in the right place. Brand development is no different. The foundations of the brand has to be in place prior to investing in the marketing mix. The foundation stones covered in this chapter are the establishment of the category, the positioning and the brand personality.

In Part 2 a couple of branding golden rules were introduced. For the implementation there is but one really golden rule and it is in one word only and that is FOCUS. Focus on the most important issues, focus on the most effective tools in the marketing mix, focus on the most important brands, focus in the positioning and establishing of the brand personality, focus in targeting, etc. Provided that brand management has done the homework in the proper way and consequently knows what to focus on, the most important thing to bear in mind is to ensure that all activities have a focus, and the same focus all across the marketing mix.

### GETTING THE CATEGORY RIGHT

One of the classical marketing questions is 'what business are we in?' Everyone who has had any form of marketing training will have heard of the example of the US train companies who thought they were in the train business when they were in the transport business. There are many other similar examples such as the initiative by the late Robert Maxwell to launch a 24-hour newspaper in London with new editions all around the clock. Unfortunately Robert Maxwell did not realize that people fulfil their craving for immediate news through radio and television while newspapers, in particular the so called tabloid press, are bought for their entertainment value.

It is a marketing axiom to state that brand management has to clearly define the product category. It is equally true that while in retrospect it is easy to spot mistakes, to correctly define the product category can sometimes be difficult. Even for well-known products the answer is not straightforward: Is Coca-Cola in the cola or soft drink category? Is Disney in the leisure, entertainment or movie business? Is Ford in the car market, family car or transport category – or in all of them and using sub-brands to be more specific?

The more distinct the category, the easier it is to position and build values, but it does restrict the potential of the brand.

## *Examples*

A real but modified case:

In the soft drinks market in one country orange drinks account for 8% of all soft drinks, the rest is mainly colas (70%) and various other fruit-based drinks. A company is about to launch a new orange drinks brand and research has indicated that this specific formula has tremendous appeal. In this case is the market orange drinks, soft drinks or non-colas? All answers might be correct depending on circumstances. In the event the non-cola category was chosen, a decision with significant influence on how to market the product.

An actual example:

Nestlé launched in the early 1990s a range of frozen prepared meals in Germany under the Findus brand. The Findus brand was chosen as it is the Nestlé brand for this type of food. For various reasons the launch was not as successful as expected so by mid-1990s the house brand was changed from Findus to Maggi. Maggi is one of Germany's strongest food brands, also owned by Nestlé, and is positioned as a food brand. By changing the house brand on the frozen food range, the company also changed the product category from frozen convenience foods to convenience foods.

The product category has of course to be defined from the perspective of the customers. To correctly define the category you have to move into the mind of the customers and assess how he/she looks at the market. In reality they often look at it in a much more simplistic way than the marketer!

For the categorization to make sense from a business as well as a marketing point of view, one more aspect has to be considered. The chosen category has to be one which the company has capabilities to compete within. It is all very well to state that the trains in the US were in the transport business but if the company does not have the capabilities of competing in the transport business, the choice of category is of no use unless investments are made to rectify the situation. In the case of the trains, this would clearly have been worthwhile but that is not always the case.

---

## *Example (disguised)*

The marketing director of a European pâté company had concluded that the company and the house brand was not only in the pâté business, it was in the savoury spreads business. The consequence of this conclusion, on the face of it perfectly logical, was that the company launched under the house brand a range of cheese spreads. The first problem was that the company did not have the manufacturing know-how, nor the facilities, so the product had to be bought-in. This made the product much less profitable. The second problem was that the efforts to sell the cheese spreads took the sales focus away from the core range. The third problem was that the marketing definition was not the consumers' definition. For the consumers the house brand was intimately connected to pâtés, i.e. products made from meat, and did not consider a cheese spread under such a brand as something of particular interest. After all, why should someone who is good at making pâtés, also be good at making something from cheese? The result, the cheese spread range was a disaster from both the volume and profit perspective and with the arrival of a new Managing Director the whole project was discontinued.

---

As illustrated above, it is essential to get the product category classification right. It is worthwhile spending considerable time on looking at various aspects and dimensions to ensure that the defined category is the correct one, but deciding on category without taking the total business situation into account is to market with blinkers.

## GETTING THE POSITIONING RIGHT

Positioning was first forcefully put on the marketing map by Al Ries and Jack Trout in their classical 'Positioning – the battle for your mind'. The term has since been used for various concepts and, of course, a brand can be positioned in many different ways. In the following I will in principle follow the Ries–Trout approach which is that the key to positioning is to have your brand take a specific position in the minds of the customers.

Positioning is mainly, still, used as a tool to develop more relevant and effective advertising. To build brands properly, positioning must take a more central role as unless all the aspects of the brand, including the functional benefits, are consistent with the positioning, the end result will be less than satisfactory. Although the intention is not to repeat Ries–Trout's theory, one aspect is worth special consideration, the concept of the ladder of the mind, which is linked to the previous paragraphs on the product category. The theory is that for each product category the customers will have a ladder of preference. One brand will occupy the top position of the ladder, such as Microsoft for PC software, Coca-Cola for soft drinks and Kodak for film, and other brands will follow, such as Lotus, Pepsi and Fuji in the three mentioned categories.

The second part of the ladder of the mind theory is consistent with the principle of being Number 1, described in Part 1, that the top brand is in the strongest position. It is very difficult to unsettle a brand which has managed to occupy the top slot because the brand at the top will always be top of mind. If you choose Microsoft you might well not consider Lotus an alternative, but if you choose Lotus you are most likely to have first considered Microsoft and then rejected it for some reason. While the situation can be manageable if you are number two, Pepsi is doing OK, to be number three, four or five can be a disaster as you will never be the prime choice and will have to fight with price cuts and other promotional techniques to get on the shopping list. The trauma of being a me-too. Please note that although the examples used are consumer goods, the same principles apply to industrial goods. It is as important to be top of mind in that sector as in the consumer goods one.

For big brands in distinct categories the pattern is simple but very few brands fall into this definition and this is where positioning and choice of category come together.

To be able to dominate the ladder of the mind, you have to define the category so that you have a chance of becoming Number 1. Volvo could never be top of the ladder (outside of Scandinavia) for cars, but then there is no longer such a category so there is no need to worry. The car market is split into several different ladders and Volvo is on the top – or close to it – in the category 'safe cars' because the position Volvo occupies in most people's minds is safety. Other examples in the car business are that BMW occupies the ladder for 'cars that are fun to drive', Ferrari for luxury sports cars and Rover for 'accessible Britishness'.

Successful positioning is, in other words, not only about finding the key word or expression for the brand but to link the expression to a ladder of the mind which is relevant to the customers and which the brand has a chance to dominate. Other factors to bear in mind are that the positioning must be distinct, as otherwise it will not be a position, the customers must see it as a credible claim or statement and ideally it should be easy to prove and demonstrate. And, also here consistency is of the utmost importance.

A single product or service brand can usually successfully be positioned by using just one word or a short sentence. A more complex product such as a retail brand, i.e. a brand covering the store fascia and the products inside often requires a more complex process. According to the Marketing Director of Sainsbury's, a leading UK grocery retailer, to differentiate a retailer brand you obviously work with the quality and choice of merchandise but also with several other dimensions. While a P&G brand can be built on one single dimension, Head & Shoulders – fighting dandruff, a retailer must work with a more complex set of variables to position itself in the market place. Our own experience with some leading retailers in other categories confirms this.

---

# *Example*

One excellent example of distinct positioning and pragmatic implementation is 'Fisherman's Friend', the small bag with throat lozenges from Lofthouse in Fleetwood on the east coast of Britain. By design or accident, the brand is positioned in an excellent way through the name and the words 'extra strong' and on the back of the little pack the product story is told, how it was created for and used by the North Sea fishermen. Fisherman's Friend illustrates that it is not necessary to have fancy, glossy packs and brochures for positioning a brand, you can also get on a small space a full product story if you use the right language. And, also a small company and brand can be successful, Fisherman's Friend is now sold in over 100 countries worldwide.

---

There are two effects of positioning which sometimes are forgotten. The first one is that a distinct positioning does mean that some aspects and targets are excluded. If in one market sector such as yoghurt no brand is distinctly positioned, then all brands will carry the generic image of yoghurts. If, however, one brand is distinctly positioned as healthy, that will appeal to some but alienate those not interested in healthy food. It will also mean that other dimensions such as good taste will get less attention. To become more competitive by a distinct positioning the brand will exclude some general aspects.

The second is that by clearly positioning your own brand, you can also reposition competition. If one yoghurt makes strong health claims, that can make the other brands seem unhealthy. If one yoghurt is low fat, the others can be seen as high fat.

Arriving at the correct positioning takes time and creativity. It requires a total understanding of the brand, the company, the competition, the market, the customers, etc. While research can tell you what the current positioning is, the positioning a brand is aspiring to is a management decision. However, management cannot decide what the customers will perceive, it can only prepare the ground on which the customers will build a positioning in their minds. But the more distinct the company is in its execution, the more likely it is that the customers will share the brand management positioning.

## GETTING THE BRAND PERSONALITY RIGHT

Not that long ago it was considered sufficient to get the USP (unique selling proposition) right for a brand, once defined everything else would take care of itself. The positioning concept demonstrated that the USP was not enough, you had to go further, position the brand in the mind of the customer. As more and more brands are positioned properly, the competitiveness has forced brand management to consider in more detail other aspects of the brand, and the brand personality is one such factor.

The brand personality can be described as the positioning's clothes. The positioning is short and distinct, the brand personality is wider and more colourful. While the positioning should not change over time, if correctly defined and implemented, the personality evolves with fashion and what is happening in the market place. The brand personality is also a reflection of the abstract brand values, and certainly consistent with them. If trust is a key value, the personality has to be easily identifiable with someone who is trustworthy.

Dimensions to bear in mind for the brand personality can be colourful, youthful and sparkly for a soft drink and solid engineering, attention to detail, economical and well-respected for a car. For a well-defined brand it is even possible to describe the people working with the brand in great detail, what kind of house they live in, what they eat and drink, what kind of family life they have, and so on. The technique to compare brands with animals or countries can also come handy. How a brand personality is described should really reflect the brand itself. If the brand symbols are fairy-tale figures, then one should write a fairy tale to describe the personality and if it is a youth brand with links to music, then describe the band and the music they are playing.

## GETTING THE CONCEPT RIGHT

The final link in getting the basics right in this context is to correctly define the communication concept. What is the key message, what is the environment of the message, which visual and literary expressions are suitable, etc.

Concept development is a creative process and the advice is to try as many directions as possible as the more directions that are explored the more likely it is to find the best solution. In one instance we developed over 200 different concept ideas to be able to define in more elaborate format about 30, which in turn resulted in ten concepts put into market research.

Contrary to the positioning, and to a degree the personality, the concept can change during the life of a brand, not every year but certainly within a five-year period. For the different concepts to be effective it is of course necessary to link them closely to the positioning and ensure that they correctly reflect, not only the positioning, but also the key brand values. But it is also possible to use concept development to establish new values and link them to the brand so that the appeal will increase.

This is, presumably, what Volvo has been doing since the mid-1990s. By stressing and developing the driving qualities of first the 850 and then S70 – and developing model variants with more power and technical features – the company is trying to create an additional brand value to the brand, one of a car fun to drive, in addition to the well-established ones such as safety and reliability. Whether this will increase the appeal of the brand – by adding a dimension – or decrease as the focus is blurred and the original ladder of safety is to a degree diminished, remains to be seen.

Traditionally the task of building the brand personality has been delegated by brand management to the advertising agency. While it makes sense to use the creative powers of an advertising agency to establish the dimensions of the personality, the issue is too important not to be part of the responsibility of brand management. Further, the brand personality is not only related to advertising, everything related to the brand builds the personality; and also brands without advertising support will benefit from having an appealing defined brand personality.

## GETTING THE TARGETING
## AND SEGMENTATION RIGHT

It is another marketing 'motherhood statement' that you have to get your targeting right. Selecting the appropriate target group is, of course, extremely important for cost-effective marketing, both in order to get the product and message right, but also to ensure that you are communicating with the right people. Targeting is one of the areas where marketing techniques have made distinct progress, many new methods have been developed and it is a safe prediction that more is to come. It is now possible to target on a great number of different dimensions, hard facts as well as attitudinal, by using generally available data as well as in-house data bases.

From this follows that you can make the targeting process as simple or as complicated as you like. It is worth noting though that targeting should be done on at least two levels, first the target group you have in mind when developing the brand, and second those, usually in addition to the former, who are actually likely to buy the product. This can be in the traditional format of defining primary and secondary groups or be more explicit, using in the first case a very precise and extremely narrow definition, such as a 30-year-old female in central London in a professional job with an income of £35,000, eats out about twice/week, buys her clothes at Harvey Nichols, etc. While the actual target group, i.e. the people who will buy the product, is perhaps not the 30-year-old females in central London but all those who would like to be in that situation, probably covering an age span of 25–50 plus a number of other dimensions.

A related piece of advice is that it is essential to like and respect the target group. Otherwise how can you develop a marketing mix with creativity and flair? In the first case, being the role model for the brand, it usually helps to have a very closely defined target. The closer it is the easier to work with and to understand in depth the preferences and aspirations. In the second case, the commercial targeting, one has to be careful to avoid too narrow a target group, just as to avoid one that is too wide.

If the target group is too narrowly defined, there might not be enough customers to go around for building a proper brand. For generating resources and management time for the development of brand values, the brand needs to have a fairly wide appeal in one aspect. Another is that for a brand to be established and registered in the minds of the customers, it does need to have an appeal among a fair number of people, be socially acceptable. After all, a person with only one friend is not really considered an attractive person.

This must not be confused with economies of scale in production or service provision which is not a restrictive factor in all market sectors due to manufacturing flexibility or service management. It is of course feasible to have total customization of the product while maintaining a widely accepted and acknowledged brand. That is after all what the famous tailors did, and still do. Customizing the suit and the actual skill in doing that was part of the brand profile. Or the fact that a bicycle can be made in 11,000,000 different versions (a claim by the National Bicycle Industrial Company in Kokubu, Japan) to fit the riders' personal preferences does not mean that these bikes cannot be sold under the same brand.

The problems with too wide a target group is well-known. The brand will become bland and ineffective as a communication tool.

Targeting and the product categorization mentioned earlier are activities closely related to segmentation. By choosing one target group and one product category you define your market segment and by definition exclude the other parts of the market, more or less depending on the circumstances.

From a segmentation point of view that is only the first step, you might decide, or realize by observing the market place, that your brand can cover several segments. It is possible that the brand can do this with the same marketing mix, in which case the segmentation is only a way of channelling communication and perhaps product. It might also be that for each segment some modifications are required, i.e. a traditional segmentation process takes place.

The intention here is not to elaborate on segmentation techniques as the subject is well-covered in most marketing text books, more to highlight two aspects often overlooked. The first one is that for any segmentation process, the cost of the segmentation has to be less than the incremental revenue generated by the segmentation. It is even advisable to ensure that the difference is significant as most companies tend to underestimate the total cost of segmentation, management time is often not included, the building of special communication and sales channels might be difficult to fully cost, and so on.

The second is that some research indicates that the more segmented a market is, the less brand loyalty. One US study indicated a difference of 10 percentage points in brand loyalty between markets with a high level of segmentation and a low level of segmentation. (The theory behind this is developed in some more detail in my book *Chaos Marketing*.)

---

## *Example*

In the period 1991–1995 the detergent market in most European countries saw the number of products increase dramatically, the main brands were sub-branded in the form of the detergent, liquid, powder and concentrate (liquid and powder plus refills) and by adding various 'premium' formulas such as 'power' or 'future'. According to traditional marketing theory this additional segmentation of the market should lead to greater customer loyalty and higher sales as each customer should be able to buy something closer to what he/she really needs. The reality was different, at least in the UK. The consumers became confused by all the various alternatives, the leading brand Persil lost the leadership to Ariel (although this could well be due to other factors) and the leading brands Ariel and Persil together lost share (reported as 1.5 and 2 percentage points respectively in 1995) to the retailers' own labels (reported as going from 13% to 17% during 1995). Compared to previous periods the fluctuations in brand share also increased. In this once fairly stable market, brand shares shifted several percentage points from one month to another.

---

The same principles apply to the business-to-business sector although the methods and detail often differ. In some instances the market segment is only one customer but a very big one and with multilayered decision making, such as a large construction project, while in other cases it is very similar to the consumer market, such as office stationery for small offices. In particular for industrial goods where customization can be a crucial competitive factor, a viable strategy can be to keep the customization on as shallow a level as possible. Differentiating where necessary but using common components and processes as far as possible.

Proper targeting is of course essential to cost-effective brand building. Segmentation is also an integral part of brand development. While one can never be too thorough in defining target groups and market segments, a warning is in place in respect of how this is done. Too many segments and too small target groups are rarely cost-effective from the brand's perspective, while too broad a target group and no attempt to segment the market is bound to fail as the brand will be too bland and uninteresting.

In one chapter it is only possible to skim the key aspects of getting the basics right. By working through the various aspects, brand management will be well-placed to brief different departments and suppliers on what is required to develop the brand. If the homework is not done properly, a lot of time, money and effort will be wasted.

# 2
# The marketing mix

The marketing mix is the company's tool to tempt the customers, to present the products and the services sold under the brand's umbrella to all potential customers in the best possible way. The marketing mix differs of course from market to market, from country to country and from brand to brand. In the following chapters the main tools will be reviewed from the perspective of building the brand. Far from everything is covered but hopefully the main points are included.

As mentioned in Part 2, the purchasing process is very different if a brand is being bought for the first time or whether it is a repeat purchase. As the repeat purchase is the most important one for most brands, the main emphasis will be on how to improve the repeat purchase rate, but also generating new customers will be considered. In reality, the two are not exclusive, what is relevant for a first time buyer is usually also appealing to a potential repeat buyer and vice versa,

In most markets the customers are rarely 100% brand loyal. This goes for consumer as well as business-to-business. And even if the actual purchasing pattern is one of 100% loyalty, the consumer or buyer who does not from time to time consider an alternative, although rejected, is a rare animal indeed, and at least in the case of a professional buyer most probably not doing a proper job.

Accepting that all customers have a menu of alternatives at hand, a brand repertoire, the main objective of the marketing mix becomes one of increasing the frequency with which your brand is chosen (see Figure 2.1). This frequency, plus of course size of purchase, will determine the sales revenue as well as the brand share of each individual brand.

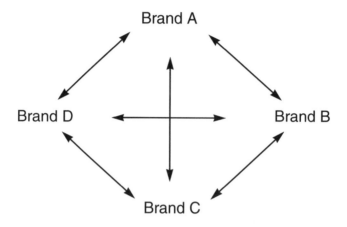

**Figure 2.1**   *The brand repertoire, alternative sequences*

In this context it is appropriate, as in Part 1, to refer to the studies made by Professor Ehrenberg and his team in London on consumer behaviour in relation to brands. Their conclusion that big brands are big because they are big is based on the fact that big brands are chosen with greater frequency than smaller brands. A simple, if perhaps frustrating, marketing axiom. In the brand repertoire, the bigger brand has an in-built advantage (in addition to usually better awareness and distribution). Contrary to popular belief the study also showed that small 'niche' brands did not have a more loyal following than the big 'traditional' brands, actually the reverse was true. The buyer of a special type of beer would also buy the main stream brands and more often than not buy more of the main stream one than of the special 'favourite' brand.

A modifying factor is that the study did not cover 'situation loyalty', i.e. that in a certain situation a consumer will prefer and choose a specific brand. This is often the case with niche brands, a special coffee for special occasions, special beer for special location and so on. Despite this the Ehrenberg conclusion remains, it is always best to be Number 1.

## MARKETING MIX – CHANGE OF FOCUS

Although the product life cycle theory is usually misunderstood and does not apply to brands (see next chapter), a market sector does go through different stages on its road to maturity and in that context the marketing mix tend to change. We first established this in the context of frozen food marketing in Europe, but the development phases have proven to be relevant to a number of different industries, within and outside of the FMCG market; although the trend is not universal and one cannot take it for granted that all new markets will develop the same way. It also applies to a much greater extent to product markets than to service ones.

For a brand to establish itself in the initial stages of a market's life, the main focus is usually on building distribution. If the sector is really new, and has a lot of appeal, the most important aspect is to get in front of the customers, gain distribution. At this stage the product offer is in the main fairly uncomplicated and product ranges are wide but not deep, i.e. different applications are covered but within each application only the most basic versions are available, although at the time they are most probably not seen as such.

Some market sectors are very slow in moving out of this phase. Beer – outside the retail trade – in the UK and in many other countries is one such market, the objective is to reach as many outlets as possible as once in the pub, the beer will be sold. Ice cream impulse items is another where in many countries the key to success is to be the brand sold in the kiosks in the good locations.

In the second phase (see Figure 2.2), the focus moves to new product development. The basic items have been distributed, presence is still important but now the offer has to be made more attractive, and the distribution system needs to be filled. New products will provide the answer. We have seen this in the personal computer market where once the computers were made readily available to the general public through computer superstores or retailer of electronic goods, the next step was to broaden the product offer.

In the third phase a much deeper understanding of the customers and a more aggressive marketing approach is required, concept marketing becomes the focus of attention. This sequence has some common characteristics with the three phases of marketing as described in Part 1. In this context there are some specific issues to bear in mind. One is that even though the focus moves to concept marketing, that does not mean that it is not important to ensure that the distribution is in place or that new products are developed as needed.

| | |
|---|---|
| **1.** | Distribution |
| **2.** | Distribution |
| | New Product Development |
| **3.** | Distribution |
| | New Product Development |
| | Concept Marketing |

**Figure 2.2**   *Marketing mix – change of focus*

Another is to comment on 'focus'. It makes sense to introduce concept marketing already at phase 1 if the company has resources. But what Figure 2.2 illustrates is that this must not be at the expense of achieving excellent distribution and, not least, that it is possible to succeed without knowing how to or worrying about concept development. The third aspect is that if you do not adapt your marketing to changed circumstances, you will be run over.

### A few general aspects

The first one is to adapt the marketing mix to each individual situation. This is self-evident but never-the-less deserves a mention as it is so often forgotten. While it makes sense to learn from other market sectors or other countries and regions, the local circumstances must always be considered.

---

## *Example*

For the frozen food market referred to earlier, the reality is that in the early stages of that market in virtually all European markets, the brand leaders held a 70–80% market share. This was sometimes held by one company and sometimes by two, usually Unilever and Nestlé. Once the market moved from being distribution dominated, the brand shares of the leaders fell dramatically from, in the case of Unilever, in excess of 50% to at the most 20% and in some instances such as UK and Germany closer to 15%.

---

This aspect is often of greater importance than generally acknowledged. When entering a market, brand management can either go against the tradition of the market or adapt to it. Either way you have to be aware of what the best practice is in the specific market and whether an alternative can be effective. Daewoo, the Korean car company, has been relatively speaking very successful by going against the traditional way of selling cars, and making a virtue out of it; while for instance in the detergents market the leaders P&G and Unilever have established a way of marketing which serves both as a barrier to entry and a blueprint for how to do it. Brands that cannot adapt to this have not been able to succeed.

The second aspect is to make sure that all possibilities for generating synergies are taken care of. For most brands there is potential for synergies at different levels. The most basic one is to ensure that all the different communication elements of the marketing mix are consistent with each other and, of course, the way to do that is to ensure that the basics first are in place, and second are followed. Synergies can also be found by co-ordinating different types of activities. To take a simple FMCG example: If a brand is featured on price promotion, a 20% discount will be less effective than a 10% discount plus some attractive point of sale material in the shops.

What is slightly more difficult to achieve but still very much worthwhile is to ensure that all parts of the company act coherently and are following the brand profile. Every contact a customer has with a company will influence the perception of the brand(s), and this includes a friendly chat in the pub by a factory worker. All the contacts build a reputation and all need to be managed for getting the most out of the company to support the brand. This applies for instance to order takers and distribution staff as well as sales staff. When visiting our local Chinese restaurant and being addressed by name as I was leaving the restaurant, 'Thank you, Mr Nilson' instead of 'Thank you, Sir', my appreciation of the restaurant, as well as the meal I had just taken, went up, encouraging a repeat purchase in the not too distant future.

Synergies can sometimes also be found between different brands of the company. This can be in a practical way when it comes to selling and distribution, but sometimes also in other respects. A coffee-vending machine in an office is made more attractive if it can offer coffee as well as a chocolate bar, a strategy followed by Nestlé with Nescafé Gold Blend coffee and KitKat bars. By utilizing synergies the brand management can make 1+1 = 3 or even 5. If synergies are ignored and activities are left to compete with each other, the result might well be 2+2 = 3.

In the same train of thought it is also worthwhile to establish that it is better to 'sail with the wind', than against. If the market trend is in one direction, it is almost always more productive to follow that trend than going against it. If a market sector is in decline, it takes a significant effort to change that pattern, while if the market is in a growth phase most new initiatives will be welcome.

## YOU HAVE TO KNOW WHAT YOU WANT TO BE ABLE TO GET WHAT YOU WANT

For brand management to get the best results from the marketing mix, the providers of the marketing services have to properly briefed. This is another marketing motherhood statement but again often overlooked or ignored.

No professional brand management should, in my view, allow any activity to build brand values unless a proper, written brief exists. This brief can be very open or very specific but unless it is committed to paper, costly mistakes are likely to follow. The cheapest way of making cost-effective marketing possible is to brief properly. What the brief should include depends of course on the circumstances, but a minimum is to include some background information, objectives and key strategies, the brand profile including positioning and personality, responsibilities and a time plan.

The marketing mix can be dynamite in the hands of skilled brand management or a golden nugget falling to the bottom of the sea if implemented the wrong way. Understanding the brand, attention to detail, commonsense and some creative flair can be excellent ingredients in creating a positive impact in the market place.

# 3
# Product development – an introduction

Product development is probably the most important part of the marketing mix. There are perhaps some exceptions to this, such as some cosmetics brands, but for most products and services, developing the actual offer is of fundamental importance. To ignore this can be foolish and is also a signal of disrespect for the customers. Thinking that a glossy communication mix or distribution power can skim over weaknesses in the delivery of the goods shows, in my view, contempt for the customer and short-sightedness in respect of the company and its owners and employees.

Successful brands constantly improve their products and services. The improvement can be in various forms and does not necessarily have to be of the traditional format, for instance it can be as effective to improve the service package going with a product as improving the product itself. The wise brand management looks at all these aspects.

For the brand's long-term strategic survival it is important to mix complex long-term projects with short-term ones. Without short-term development there will not be any business in the long term and if long-term projects are stopped the more fundamental development trends might well be missed.

Product development is necessary but can also be unnecessary or very expensive. The key to success is not to spend vast amounts on R&D but to ensure that the product or service provided is always of the best possible standard within the cost parameters, providing value for money.

Many of the most extraordinary business developments have not had their origins in traditional R&D. Microsoft, without doubt one of the greatest business successes in the 1990s is based on adaptation of ideas and, especially initially, a window of opportunity – to supply operating software to IBM's PC – which was exploited with the greatest skill.

On the other hand companies with the highest R&D spend, according to the *Financial Times* in 1996 this was General Motors (around $9 bn) and Ford (around $7 bn), are not known for any great innovations. It is also true that many great innovators have been incapable of exploiting their inventions. The use of quartz for watches was invented in Switzerland but commercialized in Japan and the US and did not benefit the Swiss industry until much later with the Swatch. The invention of the transistor in Britain did not do much good to the British electronics industry. This is not to say that R&D is not necessary. It is to point out that R&D expenditure is no guarantee for innovation and that commercial acumen seems to be more important.

Product development is traditionally split into traditional product development and process development. Developing the process of manufacture or providing a service can be as important as developing the product itself. The Japanese boom during the 1970s and to a degree in the 1980s, was to a large extent an effect of process development rather than product development. For instance reducing the time to build the car rather than changing the car itself. During this time it is claimed that process development took two-thirds of the resources in Japan, versus one-third for product development, while in the US the proportions were the reverse.

From a brand development point of view it can be as important to develop the process as the product, as the process will influence quality standards, the cost of manufacture and availability. The skills to achieve process development are firmly in the hands of people outside marketing so this aspect of product development will not be covered any further. Please note, this is not to indicate that it is not important, it most certainly is, but that it lies outside the competence of the author and most of the executives involved in brand management.

According to a detailed study of companies with a track record of successful product development (*Product Juggernauts* by Dechamps and Nayak) successful innovators:

- Keep things simple. Explore many alternatives early on and then choose the simplest and most robust route.

- Avoid risky leapfrogging. Many small jumps are better than one quantum leap.

- Experiment and validate new technology, don't use untested technology on key projects.

- Innovate in steps and don't introduce changes in too many areas at the same time.

Traditional product development can be split into two types of activities:

- new product development (NPD), and
- old product development (OPD).

Old product development is a term introduced in my book *Value-added Marketing* (1992). New product development represents the development and introduction of new products, whether under a new brand or not. Old product development is product improvement, how to make the existing product, or service, sold under an existing brand better and more attractive. Both aspects will be covered in the following two chapters.

## LEAD THE MARKET

In traditional classical marketing brand management observes the customers and then develops products suitable to the customers' needs. The shortcomings of this are explained in Part 1.

For successful product development it is essential that brand management adapts a more pro-active approach. In order to stay ahead of competition and be respected in the market place as a market leader and an expert on its sector, the company must take the lead:

**A market leader leads the market**.

Unless the initiative is with the brand management, the company will sooner or later be under threat.

One example of what might happen if market leadership in this sense of the word is neglected is Andrex, the toilet tissue brand. As described in Part 1 the brand was starved on innovation in the early 1990s, apparently to boost short-term profits, and consequently during the first half of the 1990s the brand share was declining, despite a most successful and attractive advertising campaign.

---

## *Example*

Gillette is an impressive case of brand vitalization with the help of product development. Gillette launched the first razor in 1903 so it is a brand with a long tradition. During the 1950s and 1960s wet shaving became unfashionable as electric razors took over. With the help of product innovations, coupled with appropriate communication, Gillette has regained the market initiative so that in the 1990s wet shaving is considerably more fashionable and more macho than electric shaving and the brand is in a very strong position.

---

Leading brands constantly innovate even if the product is of a perfectly good standard. As long as it can be made better, and most products can, the task is to ensure that market initiatives are taken and implemented.

## THE PRODUCT LIFE CYCLE THEORY

Within product development it is difficult to avoid the product life cycle theory, a concept made popular by Theodore Levitt in an article in the *Harvard Business Review* in the early 1960s. The concept introduced by Theodore Levitt was that all products go through several phases, development, growth, maturity and decline. The purpose of the original article was to highlight the technical changes in the market place and give advice on how to manage this process.

The life cycle theory has great emotional appeal, it puts an almost human element into products and brands and has proven to be remarkably popular among practitioners and academics. Is the theory correct? And, if so, does it apply to brand development? And in what way? To start from the macro level it seems appropriate to first review the concept from the perspective of a market sector.

Whether a market goes through life stages or not depends of course on the definition of a market. Avoiding semantics and using a fairly traditional view of what a market is, one can conclude that markets and market sectors certainly go through various stages. New market sectors start out with an introductory phase, or development stage, when the sector is being established. This can take a long time or be fairly quick depending on circumstances. They then grow and at some stage reach some sort of maturity when growth rates start to tail off.

What rarely happens is that market decline is due to factors outside the control of the management of companies in the sector. Trains did decline as a mode of transport as did passenger ships. In the first case perhaps it was inevitable as trains are not sufficiently flexible, in the latter case passenger ships have resurfaced as cruise ships.

For brand management to be aware of growing sectors makes a lot of sense. To worry too much about market sectors immediate decline can be a dangerous pastime for two reasons. Market sectors rarely decline and if companies expect markets to decline they will, the predictions become self-fulfilling. No one is prepared to invest in something that will decline so if the market is starved on product development and brand investments, the market will decline.

Food canning is an industry that has been written off several times. It is an old industry based on a patent granted by Napoleon. The arrival of frozen and chilled technology has done little to kill off the sector and the shops are still full of canned goods.

The next 'level' to consider is the life cycle's relevance for brands. The short answer is that the life cycle does not exist for brands more than you have an introductory phase when you grow the awareness and values of the brand and a more mature stage. If the brand is well-managed it will not decline. As noted in Part 1, most leading brands are much older than the companies controlling them and there is a multitude of brands over 100 years old. Not only the likes of Coca-Cola and Ford but also brands such as Ivory, Heineken, Cadbury and Tetley. If a brand declines and disappears this is totally due to mismanagement. As someone said 'The product life cycle theory is a good excuse for bad marketing'.

On a product level the cycle sometimes is a relevant concept, although this depends to a degree on the definition of a product category. The typewriter has, for instance, disappeared from many offices and been replaced by the PC's word processing programme. In one sense the product has disappeared, in another it has merely been transformed into a new format, more elaborate and with more features. In this case the brands involved failed to manage the product category, as hardly any of the typewriter brands managed the transformation from mechanics to electronics.

The one aspect where the life cycle applies is the technical execution of a product, and in the case of services, 'how you do it'. This was also what Theodore Levitt was most concerned about. Understand the technical progress within your product sector so you do not get left behind and can exploit and use new technology for progressing the company. This is the life cycle at the service of the brand, in the form of new or old product development.

The life cycle concept is best banned from the marketing dictionary. The dangers in letting brands and products slip in view of expected decline is much higher than any risk of market decline.

# 4
# New product development (NPD)

NPD is a classical area for brand managers to develop ideas and concepts. NPD is often fun, and if you are lucky, or skilled, and get it right you can get a lot of glory as the text books and magazines are full of interesting product launches.

For cost-effective brand development the picture is less rosy. NPD is important as without it there would be no products or services, but too much emphasis can be wasteful and ineffective.

## NPD – THE GOOD NEWS

Perhaps the most important aspect of NPD is that in the right circumstances and with the right products it can drive markets forward. The Internet has put a different dimension on business, the personal computer has changed the way we work in offices and the mobile phone has made contacting people a lot easier. In all these instances innovation has created new markets or new market segments.

The dynamism a new product concept can generate can be exceptional, as in the cases above, or it can come to virtually nothing. The cassette and CD for music were important new products, the digital cassette that came after has, at least at the time of writing, not been a success. The Polaroid camera was only a blip on the market and is now virtually only used by professional photographers, and the film cassette has to a large degree been hit by the traditional 35 mm film making a comeback.

In addition to the market dynamics a new product can set off it is also worth considering that customers are often interested in new products as such. A sales person with a new product will usually get a meeting with a buyer. The new product might not be that interesting but it will provide a selling opportunity for other products in the range. Equally in the consumer market, the word 'new' remains one of the most powerful messages. These are secondary reasons for NPD and theoretically wrong, but the real life experience is that these secondary effects can be very important for a brand.

Some companies take this aspect into full tactical use to build the brand. For an FMCG range, such as soups or yoghurt, to feature a number of new products every season is not considered strange, it is part of the marketing mix. Everyone who knows the market realizes that most of these products will fail, and will need to be replaced by another set of novelties the following season but it is all part of a tradition of marketing in the sector.

---

## *Example*

One supplier of chilled products to the British supermarkets planned one novelty every month over a 12-month period to establish interest in the company as a supplier and build the brand as being innovative – not with the consumers but the retailers. Obviously most of these twelve new ideas will and must fail as the space in the shops is limited, but as a brand building exercise it was considered worthwhile.

---

For a new product to succeed it should ideally be close to an existing concept but sufficiently different to avoid being a me-too. In the development of the petrol engine, the gradual innovations in improving the over 100-year-old combustion engine has been much more successful than the more innovative ideas such as the Wankel engine.

Another aspect indicated in the previous chapter is that it is not necessary to invent, innovation is much more productive. One reason is that it usually takes a long time to establish a true invention.

On the other hand an innovation can be developed within a

year. To take known technology and apply it in a new way can be an excellent means of developing new products. The Sony Walkman is one example, it is really only an application of known tape recorder technology but in a smaller format, the VHS video recorder is another where the key to success was the understanding that for the consumers perfect picture quality was less important than handling which made the cassette and leaning recording heads the successful solution.

---

## *Example*

One example is the microwave oven. This idea is apparently based on a patent from 1945 and was a derivative of the research into radar by British scientists during World War II. It then took some ten years before a workable product was developed and another ten years for it to be commercially available. A further ten years to come to a stage where it would be sold in reasonable quantities and another ten years to become an item which a large number of households would consider buying. This example is perhaps somewhat extreme but the pattern is the same for many other inventions.

---

## NEW PRODUCT DEVELOPMENT – THE BAD NEWS

The relevance of NPD to building business and brands differs from market sector to market sector, depending on the type of market, the stage of development and even cultural traditions.

In a fast growing, high-tech market, NPD can be crucial to success, in others it can be an expensive distraction. Most FMCG markets fall into the latter category. To begin with, a limited number of new products succeed. Some reports say 20%, others 25%. In these instances, success equals staying in the market for more than two years; real successes are much rarer. Despite this over 20,000 new food products are launched in the US every year, and Europe is not far behind.

For most established brands at the most 10–20% of sales come from products launched in the last five years. In some instances it is even less than 5%. These companies, confidentiality prohibits a listing, are very successful, with excellent profitability. I once worked with a company which had not launched a new product since 1936, it had excellent profitability and was still growing, mainly due to development of the service mix and other aspects of OPD.

A final argument is that new products fragment the market and tend to reduce economies of scale in production. This argument is not relevant to all industries but many are still in a situation where traditional manufacturing techniques dominate, and as such any new addition which does not bring in additional margin in excess of the cost of the additional product will be a drain on the resources.

The purpose with highlighting all this bad news is to bring up-front that NPD is not a certain route to success, it is an activity which can be very expensive and not in any way necessarily profitable. The purpose is not to state that NPD should be stopped, any brand and company needs to consider new products but do it with care and attention.

## NPD AND BRANDS

For a new product a company can either choose to launch a new brand or put the new product concept under one of the existing brands. In either case, a decision needs to be taken to establish the place in the brand hierarchy. The chapter on brand stretching is very relevant in this respect but to bring the issue closer to product development a few points are given below.

A totally new brand is, in most markets, a major expenditure and undertaking. It might be appropriate but to launch totally without any links to the house or corporate brand is very unusual. One example is the tunnel between Britain and France. When it was constructed it needed a name and it made sense to create a new brand, the Eurotunnel, and to give the train services specific brands, Eurostar for passengers travelling from London to Paris or Brussels and Le Shuttle for the car transport system. Another example is Direct Line, an insurance company owned by The Royal Bank of Scotland. Direct Line was, at the launch, very different from any other insurance company so it made sense to set it totally apart from any existing structure.

Later competitors have adapted a different approach, connecting the new service to the existing company such as 'Eagle Star Direct' for the direct selling arm of Eagle Star. In this case presumably the consideration has been that to differentiate from Direct Line, to avoid the cost and time of building a new brand and to use the new service to protect Eagle Star business, a closer link is better.

When the new product is closer to existing activities, and it is in the interest of the company to present it as such, a link to the corporate can be advisable. It can be as a new house brand with corporate endorsement; a new range brand with house brand endorsement; or in the case of line extensions a new product variant under the range brand.

It is impossible to establish any set rules for what is most appropriate. The first consideration must be in respect of the customers' view. How will the customers see this new product? Does it makes sense to establish a new house brand? Well, only if the new product is very new and different. Does it makes sense to establish a new range brand? This might be more likely, a really new innovation within an existing structure can warrant the development of a new range brand. For line extensions the question is easier to answer, they usually fit nicely into the existing framework, if not then they are not really line extensions.

The other aspect to ensure cost-effectiveness is to consider whether the new product concept warrants the investment into a new house or range brand. If the company cannot invest and the concept does not fit comfortably in an existing brand structure, the conclusion should be to stop the launch. There is little benefit in putting something on the market to compete with established brands, if no funds will be available for a proper launch. A product with a name does not make a brand. Perhaps a regional roll-out generating sufficient funding along the way can be a solution?

For NPD to be productive it needs to be fully integrated into the brand plans. For projects related to existing brands, decisions need to be taken so that the product fits into the brand hierarchy and the new product adds value to the brand and does not distract. If the venture is totally new, the planning should include a preliminary plan on how to brand it, prior to too much time and effort being spent on product development. By taking this into consideration and carefully balancing NPD and OPD a company can be very successful in product development.

# 5
# Old product development (OPD)

The importance of OPD is apparent to anyone closely involved in the brand development process. To ensure that the brand maintains its attractiveness, it is essential that the product or service offered is of the highest possible standard and that is only possible by OPD, improving the product performance in various ways.

The importance of this is also apparent from reviewing leading brands. It has already been mentioned that leading brands are old brands, for instance the top twenty leading brands in the UK grocery market has an average age of over 60 years. The old brands will only stay big if they are taken care of and the offering is improved. This improvement can be taken care of by constantly replacing the product portfolio or by enhancing the existing products. The successful brands do both, more or less. The products sold under the same twenty leading grocery brands have an average age of over 30 years which indicates a strategy of blending the two approaches, and when studying the brands in detail this is confirmed.

Some brands maintain almost the same product portfolio, improving the formula over and over again. Nescafé and Heinz Baked Beans from the 'top 20 list' are examples of this. Others have a strategy of launching new concepts under the house brand. Gillette razors is probably the best exponent for this strategy.

## *Example*

Tetley Tea Bags is an excellent example of OPD. Up until 1988 Tetley was the number two in the UK tea market, several points behind the leader PG Tips from Brooke Bond, part of Unilever. Although the tea market is very big (£700 million at the time), tea is still the Brits' favourite hot drink, it was a market considered dull by most marketers. The tea bags sold in the UK are different from those in most other countries as they are (or were) square and without any string attached. A cost-effective way of packing tea and one that had been used for a long time.

As part of a strategy to vitalize the brand and company, Tetley in 1987 set up an innovation programme to generate ideas. One of the ideas was a round instead of square tea bag.

To avoid the idea being copied, the development programme was carried out in total secrecy and the retail trade was only notified the week before the actual launch. Something that was made possible by the fact that the round tea bag replaced the square one, it was not a new product which required administrative changes in the stock control and pricing systems.

By changing from square to round tea bags, Tetley gained around five percentage points in market share, went from being the constant number two to brand leader and vitalized the total tea bag market in the process. Despite competitors later copying the round bag Tetley is still at the time of writing brand leader in the sector. The imitators gained nothing or very little by changing shape, only Tetley as they were the first ones.

The success of Tetley is very difficult to explain in rational terms and no well-founded explanation has been given to its success. Perhaps it is totally a question of emotion, a round tea bag is much 'nicer' than a square one.

The success of the round tea bag triggered not only imitators but in due course also other initiatives. PG Tips, the brand that lost the leadership launched in 1996 a pyramid tea bag on a regional basis. One year after the launch the conclusion by market observers was that the pyramid will not replicate the success of the round bag, as total PG Tips brand share gap to Tetley did not change significantly. Another initiative came from Tetley in 1997 in the form of a tea bag with drawstring so that the consumer can easily squeeze the drops out of the bag to avoid dripping. What lasting impact this will have on the market cannot be assessed at the time of writing but any immediate changes to the brand shares did not take place.

A dull market has been vitalized by OPD and a number two brand became Number 1 by changing the shape of the product.

Why is OPD a more successful route to follow for product development than NPD? In one sense the question is unnecessary, at least in mature markets the empirical evidence speaks for itself but to shed some more light on the phenomenon the following can be of relevance.

With OPD activities you are certain of consumer trial. With a new product one of the main problems is to get the customers to try the product. If the changes are made to an existing product, the existing customers are extremely likely to try the new, improved version.

A second aspect is that with OPD many of the variables in the product development process remain the same. In the case of the tea bag everything remained the same except the shape. This means that the company will continue to deal with known entities; it will not be necessary to have many new routines and running-in times are perhaps not eliminated but at least reduced. The 'knowing how to do it' factor is often neglected but can have significant impact on the bottom line as mistakes are less likely to happen and this contributes to the financial success of OPD initiatives.

A third set of reasons refers to economies of scale. With improving existing products instead of launching new ones, the company avoids product proliferation which costs money in the form of shorter production runs, extra stock holding and administration costs, etc. It also means that the existing, presumably high volume products will get even higher volumes which again will impact on profits.

Perhaps the most important part of the economies of scale argument is that OPD fully utilizes previous investments in the brand. Everything with the brand remains the same but only delivered in a better way. The brand will be enhanced by OPD rather than potentially split by NPD.

Most leading FMCG companies have a strong element of OPD in the marketing mix, but the strategy is also applicable to service companies. In this context it is worthwhile noting that OPD is not only about traditional product development but also improving the service, the way the product is presented and how it is made available to the public. McDonald's is one example of OPD focused on execution. It is also an example of improving and not inventing.

## *Example*

The pattern was set by the original two McDonald brothers in San Bernadino in southern California. The original McDonalds had started their first restaurant already in 1937 but the big change did not come until 1948 when they revamped their restaurant and turned it into a hamburger-only outlet with disposable cutlery. The brothers offered a standardized product, excellent quality and good value as they sold hamburgers at roughly half price of competition. The key to the value proposition was standardized processes and tools, a concept that was taken over and further developed by Ray Kroc who bought the McDonald's franchise in 1955.

The birth of McDonald's and the growth to become the world's largest food service organization and one of the world's best known brands under the leadership and inspiration of Ray Kroc, was achieved without any real block-busting innovation. The hamburger traces its origins back to the turn of the century, the fast food concept was far from new in 1948, and the use of disposables instead of proper cutlery was no novelty either. Not even the BigMac when introduced in 1968 was an invention. It was the idea of a franchisee who inspired by the success of a competitor (Big Boy) developed his own version. Most observers conclude that the reason for McDonald's success is the ability to deliver a standardized, quality, value-for-money product in attractive and clean surroundings quickly.

That OPD is an essential part of building a brand is hopefully obvious. What is not self-evident is how the improvements are communicated. Two FMCG examples can provide an illustration.

## *Examples*

Heinz Baked Beans is a British staple item, around 400 million cans sold each year generating consumer sales in excess of £120 million. The beans are also sold in other parts of the world and of course in the home market US.

The product was introduced in the UK at the turn of the century as Heinz Pork in Baked Beans, the original formula. Since then the consumers have only noted two changes to the product. The first one was in the early part of the twentieth century when the original glass jar was exchanged for a can. The second one was during World War II when the pork was taken out of the product due to rationing. The pork was never put back in as Heinz apparently noted that the product sold as well without pork as with it, so why put back an expensive ingredient?

In reality the product has gone through several other changes. The most recent one was that sugar and salt content was reduced during the 1980s to prevent health criticism and to adapt to changing taste preferences. Over a six-year period the content was gradually reduced in such a way that the consumers would not notice the difference. The reason for this strategy was that Heinz understood that baked beans are so entrenched in the British way of life that most would not appreciate any change. Why change something you have eaten all your life?

The Heinz decision was obviously right as the brand continues to do well despite competitive products being available at one-third of the price of Heinz.

The introduction of New Coca-Cola illustrates what can happen if you do not take sufficient care in the communication process when changing the product formula. The case is well-known so only the main part of the story will be mentioned here. The background is that during the early 1980s Coca-Cola saw itself under constant pressure from Pepsi, in particular in the retail trade in the US. In 1985 Coca-Cola announced the arrival of New Coke with a revamped taste, slightly sweeter presumably to be more competitive with Pepsi.

The consumers did not like the new version at all, although detailed pre-launch product testing had shown the new formula to be preferred. After public uproar the old formula was back as 'Classic' Coke and the two versions were sold side by side.

The New Coke incident was quickly repaired by Coca-Cola and the company demonstrated its admirable ability to implement change once the problem was recognized. Today the company is stronger than ever before with a market value in 1997 of almost $150 bn.

The Coke case has several learning points. First, if a product is marketed as one with a secret, never-changing formula, you should not change that formula unless there are some very good reasons. Second, if you do change a product that is dearly loved and is almost an icon, do not tell anyone. If you do not tell them, you not only avoid a communication problem, you can revert if the experiment is not working and, above all, you can change gradually. Third, if you do feel that there is a need for formula adjustment, do not copy the number two brand if you are Number 1. A market leader should lead the market, and certainly not follow number two. In this particular case Pepsi had for some time run the Pepsi taste challenge but as most food and drink market researchers know, a sip taste test comparison is not relevant as a proper comparison and a sweeter drink will almost always win in such a situation.

In my view the Coke versus Pepsi problem should not have been tackled by OPD. It would probably have been better handled by a secondary or fighting brand and in particular by making Coke stronger. If any product modification was necessary (and it should probably not be to make the product closer to Pepsi anyway), it should have been done gradually and without telling the public as there was no need to do so. This is not to neglect the consumer, it is to respect their attitudes and at the same time take action to lead the market.

OPD is an essential part of the development of any brand. To avoid improving the product or service is to stand still which of course in reality is to fall behind. For OPD to be effective it needs to be carried out in harmony with the brand values. The key values of the brand must be the focus of attention for OPD. If a key brand value is reliability, this must be constantly improved, or if it is technical supremacy, the OPD efforts must demonstrate that this is really the case. OPD is a broad concept and the more complex the products and the more similar the competitive products are, the more important it is to look at the whole value spectrum to ensure that all aspects are being reviewed for improvement to ensure customer over-satisfaction and a product superior to competition.

# 6
# Communication – an introduction

The brand developer has two sets of tools at his/her disposal, product development to enhance, primarily, the tangible brand values and communication to build the abstract values. As mentioned earlier there is an element of cross-over between the two different types of values and sometimes the enhancement of a tangible benefit might have most impact on the abstract value (if a consumer retail product is made tamper proof that will mainly boost the trust and reliability brand values, not the product performance). On the other hand feature-related communication can have as its main effect highlighting some tangible aspect of the product or service, without actually building any abstract values as such. In the main, however, product development builds tangible and communication abstract brand values.

Brand communication has two main roles, to attract attention to the brand and to build the brand profile. The two objectives will be differently balanced depending on the market position of the brand, if awareness is low attracting new customers is the main objective; if it is a well-established brand the main concern is probably more to enhance the brand position, ensuring that the brand is seen as more attractive than the competitive ones.

The more intensive and developed a market place is, the more work has to go into ensuring that a brand has a specific and distinct profile. To be able to cut through and be seen and heard among a multitude of other companies and brands, a distinct brand profile is an essential starting point. The reason is simply that someone with character is better remembered than someone who is seen as bland and grey.

Brand communication can take many different forms. The main ones will be outlined in the following chapters but the list is far from comprehensive, each market sector is different so the following is to be seen as examples and suggestions, not a complete handbook. This applies also to the emphasis that is put on each form of communication, in some instances personal selling is the main tool, in others it is advertising.

The necessity for a clear and distinct brief was outlined in Part 3, Chapter 2. While this is a relevant point for all marketing mix activities, it is of particular importance in the case of communication projects. First, many communication activities are planned and executed by marketing services companies rather than in-house staff which, in theory and often in practice, means that the involved staff are less knowledgeable about the brand. Second, communication is in many cases a subjective matter and in order to bring at least an element of objectivity and keeping the decision-making process on the right track, it is strongly advised to ensure that objectives, positioning and other crucial matters are agreed prior to starting the creative process.

The development of an effective communication strategy is at the core of successful brand building and how to do it is part of many marketing text books, thus only a brief mention is made here. By clearly thinking through the communication process ahead of briefing and ensuring that all key aspects are well-defined, much time will be saved and the end result will be better. Target group, communication objectives, brand positioning, personality, values and properties (colours, symbols, claims, etc.), the main message and considerations re the communication channel all need to be taken into account and defined so that it makes sense, utilizes all opportunities for synergies and will allow a cost-effective production and implementation. It is also advisable to define at this stage, if not done before, the follow up systems and evaluation criteria.

As with the total marketing mix, it makes sense to review the existing best practice within the market sector, either in order to adapt to it or to break it. Many large leading brands follow a similar marketing mix year in and year out with great success. So to stick to the rules of the game does not have to be the wrong strategy. But it is not necessary and if you do break the pattern, do it in a sensible way. Steve Henry of London advertising agency HHCL, and a leading exponent for breaking rules such as with the very successful Tango soft drink advertising, noted that one should not break all the rules, at least not at the same time, and picking the right rules to break is a key challenge.

---

## *Example*

British Airways in 1997 announced changes to the design of the tail fins of BA's aircraft. An example of breaking the rules within the rules. The tail is traditionally the place for the logo of the airline, how an aircraft is identified. BA changed this by replacing the old logo with a set of identities from around the world, communicating the main theme of BA which is 'the world's favourite airline'. By breaking the mould of the traditional flag-carrying national airline, BA put itself on the map in a very effective way as *the* international airline. The fact that the decision generated a lot of debate and publicity did not damage the communication effect at all, rather the reverse.

# 7
## Personal selling

Since the advent of the modern brand in the nineteenth century, the focus on brand communication has been advertising and other forms of mass communication. The national advertising campaign is, in the eyes of many, the symbol of brand marketing.

This is of course not true, all aspects of the marketing mix are important but the cliché has meant that the sales person as a marketing tool has been written off on numerous occasions but he/she is still there. The reason is that there is no more effective communication than face-to-face. You can explain, you can elaborate, you can have a dialogue, you can 'read' the customers reactions and you can customize your message. Personal selling is the ideal relationship marketing tool but with one major drawback and that is that it is expensive, sometimes very expensive.

How to manage a sales force differs very much from brand to brand and market, to market and it is a far too broad a subject to even touch on in this book.Instead the focus is on how to look at personal selling from the perspective of building brands.

As indicated above correctly managed, personal selling can be immensely powerful and it is really only the cost aspect, at both the sellers' and buyers' end, which has led to restrictions in the hiring of sales representatives. It is not only that a sales representative is expensive, the customers do not always have the time to receive them due to pressure of business.

In this respect it is worth noting that it is not only the traditional sales executive who is a sales representative. The service engineer, the order taker and the service provider are all sales representatives, if not in name, certainly in spirit.

The traditional, often caricatured, image of a sales person is one of great personality and immense powers of persuasion. Such a sales person is not necessarily the best promoter of a brand as rule number one for the selling of a brand is that the sales person must be the servant of the brand. This requires self-discipline and strict management.

Being the servant of a brand means that the individual must have a very thorough understanding of the brand and what it represents. This is, of course, important in order to present the product or service but also as the sales person represents the brand and as such must in all aspects communicate the brand values. Dress, manners and behaviour must be consistent with the brand values. If trust and reliability are key brand values, the sales representative must behave in a trustworthy way and always keep his/her promises. If the brand is a high-tech one, the sales person cannot drive in an old, badly kept car, dress in the fashions of ten years ago and use a tired pen and crumbly note-book. He/she will have to use a laptop computer, be dressed in a smart way and drive a car of the latest model (not necessarily an expensive one, though).

For a company with its own sales force this usually does not create much of a problem as the culture of the company, and thus the behaviour of the sales executives, is probably consistent with the brand values. If the company uses agents and other external sales resources the issue requires much more attention.

So to understand the brand is important and to sacrifice personality for the brand is essential. The former probably easy to implement, the latter somewhat more difficult.

The third point is consistency. Consistency is important in all aspects of brand building but if the carriers of the brand values are on the road away from head office and away from management for four days out of five, the management of consistency is a major challenge. Sales training, follow up and various team-building activities are just some ways of achieving this.

With consistency goes focus. For a sales process to be effective it has to be focused, getting to the point, getting acceptance and closing the sale. The brand values provide the focal point and the skills of the sales person will determine how well this focus is adapted to the customer's situation, developing customer focus within the brand focus.

Personal sales has always been an expensive way of selling products and services and over time the costs have increased while other communication methods have in many instances got less expensive. This is one reason for more pressure on sales executives and a reduction in numbers, and why personal selling is now fairly rare in consumer products. It is only in some high cost item markets where you find sales executives actually visiting, 'cold-calling' customers. The main focus for personal selling is the business-to-business market. Another reason for change is that the quality of buyers has in most industries increased over time and if the quality of the buyers increase, the quality of sellers has to keep pace, or preferably stay one step ahead.

The change has probably been most dramatic in sales to the retail trade. Only some twenty years ago the leading suppliers to the retail trade would have in the UK 300–400 sales representatives. Today, you can manage with ten to cover 60–70% of the trade and with 40–50 you can serve the country. The trend is the same in many other countries. The other aspect of this trend is that the remaining sales executives have to be more skilled and be able to represent the brand in a totally different way as it requires different skills to sell to the current target – such as the head buyer of a large supermarket chain – than the former, as an example a shop manager or the owner of a corner shop.

At the other end of the retail trade, at the front end in the contact with the consumers, personal selling remains in many instances very important. The numbers are, of course, lower now with various self-service systems in place (at Safeway grocery stores in the UK you even do your own scanning of goods, 'jumping' the queue at the check-out) compared to 50 years ago but most retailers have realized that a store without human service is not an attractive place to shop.

All the principles mentioned in this chapter in relation to the traditional sales representative are applicable to retail staff as well. All need to communicate with the consumers according to the brand values, be aware of customer needs and be focused in the sales process. The retail brand management who ignores this aspect of brand building, or just does not pay sufficient attention to training and information, is doing the brand and business a great disservice.

Many marketing executives have a love-hate relationship with the sales force. They love the sales force because it is important for achieving targets, they hate it because most sales representatives are sometimes difficult to persuade, or it seems that way. The reason is often that the sales people need to voice all objections early on so that they know how to handle any questions, and of course, the need to subordinate personal profile for the brand profile is not always easy to accept.

From the marketing perspective one aspect is important to remember and that is the fact that a good product or service, i.e. a product that is well-presented, well-positioned and branded, with good support and a set of values which appeals to the customer base, is the sales person's best friend. If the proposition makes sense, the sales force will love it, if not then there is either a problem with the proposition or the presentation. In other words, if the love-hate relationship exists, the reason might well be substandard brand management.

The personal selling process remains one of the most powerful ways of communicating with the customer base but for it to be a cost-effective process it must also be properly targeted to those customers where the potential for sales will justify the expense. The challenge for brand and sales managements is to ensure that the sales process is focused, consistent and that the individuality of the sales force becomes a powerful servant of, and not a parasite on, the brand values.

# 8
# Sales promotion

Sales promotion is a necessary part of the marketing mix for most, if not virtually all, brands. The brand management that does not have to find ways of promoting its brand due to competitive pressure is a rare animal, or operates in an environment where sales promotion is not possible, such as major construction projects.

The purpose of sales promotion is to generate a sales uplift by temporary measures. The challenge is to achieve this in a way that the sales uplift is not countered after the promotion by a sales decline so that the net effect is zero, and that the activities actually build brand perceptions and not devalue the brand.

When planning and deciding on sales promotion activities it is important to pay attention to the setting of objectives. On the face of it the objective should always be to increase short-term sales but that may not always be the case. The objective can be to promote brand values for long-term sales effects or, at the other end of the spectrum, it can be a way just to cut through the noise level, not necessarily increasing sales, only promoting to stand still. And, closely related to this is the objective to promote in order to make the sales force pay attention to the product, not even getting through the customers' noise level but the internal one.

For the marketer searching for new promotional ideas, the suggestion is to look at what has been done before, try to find a different application and run the promotion again. Most promotional ideas were already created by the 1930s so to find something totally new will be very difficult. To find a new application is much easier and also more likely to be successful.

## PRICE PROMOTIONS

Sales promotion is traditionally divided into price-related and non-price promotion.

The price promotion has many advantages. It is easy to administer, you just put in a discount, it is easy to communicate, everyone understands what a price cut is all about and you can fairly easy follow the progress so that you know where you are in respect of costs.

On the other hand there are many disadvantages as well. From a brand development perspective the most important one is to assess what kind of impact it will have on the brand values. Other negative aspects are that it is easy to copy so if one company reduces the price, the next one can follow the next day and you often need to reduce the price by a fairly substantial amount in order to get a sales uplift which means that the risks of losing rather than gaining revenue can be quite high.

Just because a promotion is price related does not mean it has to be a traditional price off or coupon activity.

## *Example*

A co-operation between Flora, a margarine, and BT, British Telecom, resulted in utilizing an old-fashioned technique, collection scheme, in a new way. The promotion, communicated on the Flora packs, involved the consumer collecting a number of Flora lids. The consumers mailed the lids to Flora and in return got a reduction on the phone bill. In addition to the novelty value, at least in the UK, the consumer was twice hit by a positive message. First, when collecting the lids and realizing that he/she could save money and second, when receiving the phone bill where the saving from Flora was highlighted.

Temporary price reductions can impact the brand values in two different ways. First, there are those close to economic theory and pure value-added marketing and second, aspects more related to the building of brand values. In theory, if the price is reduced and with it the perceived price, the product or service should become more attractive and with it the appeal of the brand. How a customer will react depends on a number of factors such as the type of product, usage patterns, and whether the product is new or not.

While it is difficult to generalize regarding the relevance for different types of products, it is easier to assess the other aspects. A product which is used with some frequency, has additional usage applications and where customers usually buy more than one brand, is more likely to respond positively to price promotions than one where this is not the case.

It is also so, contrary to popular belief but proven in several cases, that a new product is more likely to respond favourably than a well-established one. The reason is, of course, that if additional penetration can be gained, and the product or service provides good perceived value – over-satisfying the customers – the new customers will continue to buy also when the product is back to normal price.

Some research also indicates that for products and brands in decline, price promotion tends to increase the decline rather than reducing it. This goes against many marketers' intuition but the reason is probably that first, it is unlikely that any new customers will be converted, second, that the lower price will devalue the already weak brand values thus making the product seem to be worth less and finally, more doubtful, perhaps the lower price is seen as a signal that the brand is on its way out – and who wants to buy something that no one wants. The reality of these conclusions has been experienced by those trying to sell out remaining stock of an old product, it can be a very difficult task.

The second aspect of this is how the price reduction impacts on the brand value spectrum. A reduced price point can give a signal that this product is substandard and thus reduce the brand values and consequently future sales could be hurt. Whether this is true or not is in my view not sufficiently proven. Until we know better, the advice is to ensure that price promotions are handled with care.

The brand value can also be affected by the fact that a price promotion will draw attention to the price as such. Price awareness differs across markets and price promotions will of course make customers more aware of the price level and perhaps start comparing to a greater degree.

A result of price promotions in the FMCG market that is sufficiently proven is that the main part of brand switchers due to price promotions will switch back again if other brands in the sector also price promote. The customers attracted by a price cut usually remain only short-term users of the brand. Given the comment above regarding new products this applies in particular to established product categories.

The heavy price promotions in some FMCG markets have led some brand companies such as P&G in the US, to operate a 'every day low price' strategy, i.e. no temporary price promotions but a lower on-going price. The reason for this is to avoid the additional costs of short-term price promotions such as the impact on stocks and cost of coupon handling. As the objective here is not to go into detail but rather to highlight specific features, the conclusions appear to be that the strategy works for brand leaders but is a less advisable strategy if you are number two or three.

Price promotion in the retail industry is in most cases a very important factor as it serves not only the purpose of boosting sales but also to build a brand value of 'value for money'. The difference between a retailer and a manufacturer is mainly due to the fact that a retailer can use a limited number of items to demonstrate a value profile, while this is of course not possible for a product-based brand. It is worth noting, though, that the strategy appears to be effective only if executed, as one would expect, in harmony with brand values.

The reality of price promotion is that it is very difficult not to price promote if other competitors are doing it; in many markets it is a way of life. For a new product or service it can be an effective method, but for old declining products (presumably already mismanaged from a brand development point of view) it will do little, if any, good and a good follow up system is strongly recommended.

## NON-PRICE PROMOTIONS

While there are very few truly new ideas in sales promotion, the usage of technology in combination with focused creativity has produced some interesting developments. For a promotion to be effective it ideally has to relate closely to the core values of the brand, but it can be a simple idea or a very elaborate one.

---

## *Examples*

An example of the former is a ready wrapped After Eight chocolate box for Christmas. The pack is displayed on the shelves already wrapped with a removable sticker holding all the necessary product information. The customer only needs to remove the label to have a handy present. The promotional pack is only sold in selected outlets such as duty-free shops due to restrictions in selling packs with peelable labels in general trade.

A more elaborate promotional concept was developed for Tango, the UK orange soft drink. The Tango advertising is most unusual and of a very high creative standard. One device used in the 1996 advertising was an orange rubber doll. The doll provided the centre piece for a promotion where the consumers, in the main teenagers, could phone in to Tango, answer some 'Tango-ish' questions and as a reward receive the doll. The whole promotion was self-liquidating as the cost of the telephone call paid for the doll and postage. By presenting the promotion in the right way, and understanding the target group, Tango managed to no cost distribute a great number of brand symbols and no doubt created a lot of attention and sales in the process.

In 1997 the exercise was repeated but this time the gadget was an old-fashioned horn, presumably much enjoyed by teenagers!

---

A more traditional but almost always very effective way of promoting products in the business-to-business sector is to combine promotions with corporate hospitality. For big or otherwise important customers to visit interesting production sites or to learn more about a product and the market can be very effective. Customers are, as a rule, interested in learning more about how to use products, to understand them better and find new applications, and if this can be combined with competitions or other types of promotions, a number of objectives can be fulfilled at the same time.

Most effective non-price sales promotion activities are linked to some distinct aspect of the brand and/or the advertising. They are also often run as self-liquidating activities which makes them more financially viable.

---

## *Example*

Nescafé Gold Blend (in US Taster's Choice and in continental Europe sometimes called Gold, Lyx, Luxus or Special Filtre) is a leading brand in the instant coffee sector in the UK. Gold Blend advertising is based on a 'love story' which in many ways has caught the imagination of the British public, and also successfully been translated into many other markets. On the basis of the advertising success, Nestlé has produced and sold Gold Blend records with romantic music, the Gold Blend book with the full story to read at home, etc. All activities successfully building the brand.

---

For all marketing activities it is essential that the logistics are in place to handle the programme and this is particularly so in sales promotion.

---

## *Example*

One by now classical example of how not to do it is Hoover UK offering free flights to the US in return for buying a vacuum cleaner in the autumn of 1992. The downfall of the promotion was that insufficient care was taken in ensuring that low-priced tickets were available and the company underestimated the appeal of the promotion. The promotion certainly did sell many vacuum cleaners but to a very high cost of £48 million and immense badwill to such an extent that several top executives had to leave the company and the company was in the end sold by the owner Maytag.

---

Another example is a mobile phone company offering free phone calls over the Christmas period. The customers found the offer so attractive that the whole phone system jammed and created badwill instead of goodwill.

A sales promotion technique much used is various on-going

collection schemes, such as store cards or air miles programmes. Many of these were set up as promotional schemes but as they are on-going and not temporary and have many other uses, the concept is dealt with under 'relationship marketing'.

Successful sales promotion has to be consistent with the brand values and be consistent with all other aspects of the brand. This is worth noting as it is easy to get excited over an idea in itself but it might on closer examination not match the brand criteria. The trend in recent years towards fewer promotions and a higher quality is equally of value as for a promotion to go beyond getting the internal sales force and the most dedicated and brand loyal buyer excited, something extra is required. If the extra brand boost is not achieved, the whole promotion is wasted.

# 9
# Advertising

Advertising is what most brand managers aspire to getting involved in. It is an activity still surrounded by exciting imagery and the dream for many is to be involved in a campaign that really makes a difference. Few manage this as not many brands are sufficiently big to warrant an advertising budget which will provide resources for a big campaign and in reality, and absolutely correctly given the sums involved and the relevance to brand building, advertising is such an important activity that it should be the responsibility of brand management, not brand managers.

One communication challenge which is particularly relevant to advertising is to ensure that it actually works. The old saying of 'half my advertising is wasted but I don't know which half' is not totally irrelevant, according to Professor J P Jones in his book *When Ads Work* the success rate is 46%. As with the other elements of the marketing mix the intention is not to cover the subject of advertising in its totality but merely to focus on some relevant issues regarding how to add values to brands. For more facts on when advertising works, or not, Professor Jones' book mentioned above is recommended and for more qualitative information advertising guru David Ogilvy's *Ogilvy on Advertising* is a good source and inspiration.

Although classical mass advertising is the prerogative of only a few mega brands, the craft of creating good advertising is important for many others as well. One reason is that in many markets it is not necessary with million pound or dollar budgets to achieve results, many brands have been launched on much smaller budgets. Another reason is that even if your brand is not advertised you still need to have a thorough understanding of advertising because it is an important part of the commercial environment. Someone has calculated that the average 35-year-old British adult will have seen 150,000 commercials, many of them more than six times. The effect of this is that all customers, whether in the consumer or business-to-business market, are advertising literate and have developed an understanding of mass communication.

It is not necessary with large budgets to achieve striking results, it just more difficult.

## *Examples*

A classical example often quoted by David Ogilvy is his advertisement for Rolls-Royce in the US. Rolls-Royce is admittedly not the average kind of brand but never-the-less with one press advertisement execution with the headline 'At 60 miles an hour the loudest noise in this new Rolls-Royce comes from the electric clock' followed by thirteen good reasons for buying a Rolls-Royce, the brand was placed on the map of buyers of luxury cars. The advertisement only ran in two newspapers and two magazines at a total cost of $25,000. Not much but do note that this was when a Rolls could be bought for $13,995.

A more recent example is the launch campaign for Häagen-Dazs ice cream in the UK. In 1990 Häagen-Dazs was unknown and the premium ice cream sector small. The objective of Häagen-Dazs was to establish itself in the market with a product selling at a 50% premium to the nearest premium ice cream competitors.

The Häagen-Dazs advertising broke the mould of featuring luxury ice cream in exclusive surroundings. The key brand value was defined as sensual, expressed in the brief as 'the ultimate in intimate pleasure' and in the advertisements (mainly press) as 'Dedicated to pleasure' with very sensual, almost erotic, illustrations.

According to published information the total media spend was less than £500,000 (a share of total ice cream advertising of 6%) but the campaign made Häagen-Dazs a very well-known brand, sales increased dramatically to make the brand the leader in the sector with a share of around 30% in early 1992.

The Häagen-Dazs example is fairly well-known, it is an excellent example of building a brand, creatively positioning a product in a new way and in reality becoming a marketing bench-mark. But a good brand is not necessarily also a good business. In the case of Häagen-Dazs the published accounts for Häagen-Dazs (UK) Ltd show a reported loss of £3.7 million (28.8% of sales) for 1992 and £6.0 million (27.2%) in 1993.

For an outside observer it seems that Häagen-Dazs managed to overcome the challenge of getting noticed and create a brand with strong values with only a limited budget but failed in other aspects of the business, where perhaps the economies of scale were more difficult to overcome.

Why do companies advertise? Some companies have well-defined objectives, others do it just because they think it is a good idea, the customers like it or everybody else is doing it. Traditional advertising, as well as most other types of communication, has to fulfil three different roles.

First, it has to announce that a product or service is available, let the customers know that it exists. In this sense advertising is basically replacing the shouts of the street trader. To achieve this, the advertising has to be noticed, get attention and awareness for the brand. There is of course little point in having advertising noticed but the brand and product forgotten. During the late 1970s Cinzano ran a series of commercials in the UK featuring not only the famous actor/comedian, Leonard Rossiter, but also Joan Collins. Unfortunately the advertising became more famous than the brand and it is claimed the competitor Martini gained more from the advertising than Cinzano.

The second role is to inform, to go one step beyond announcing, letting customers know that this brand exists and the product or service will do this or that, in short communicate the tangible values and benefits of the brand. To go back to the comparison with the street trader, this is when the trader shouts 'perfectly ripe, excellent bananas from the Caribbean' instead of just 'bananas'. Many marketing and advertising executives live very close to their brands so they sometimes forget that not everybody is aware of the products they are advertising. It should also not be forgotten that many customers enter the market place every year and people forget. The brand does not exist which is well-known by everybody so it is essential that the advertising informs. To what degree is, of course, another matter and differs from campaign to campaign depending on communication objectives.

The third role is to build a personality and create long-term brand values, primarily the abstract ones. This is the most difficult aspect but should never be ignored. All really good examples of advertising fulfil all three roles.

The degree of brand building advertising can achieve depends both on the product, the market place and the target group. In some areas, such as Levi's jeans, Nike and many beer brands, the advertising takes on a very important role as one key brand value is to reflect and 'hi-jack' for the brand the values of the target group's aspirational role models. On other occasions, the advertising takes more the role of reminder and features the product's tangible values, P&G's doorstep challenge for Daz being a prime example. (The doorstep challenge is, in short, that a brand spokesperson challenges a person on the doorstep to swap his/her regular detergent for Daz, leaves a pack and then comes back later to record that Daz is now the favourite.)

Advertising can also take a more business planning role, especially for big brands. By spending large amounts on advertising, brands can create barriers to entry, make it more difficult for competitors to get established as small brands cannot afford a big budget. The approach is mainly relevant to consumer markets and detergents is one such market sector where this seems to apply.

What kind of expenditure is, generally speaking, required to increase brand share with the help of advertising? Research indicates that to increase brand share, a company would need a share of voice significantly over the brand share, to move from 10% to 15% brand share the company would need a share of voice of perhaps 20–25%. In other words, advertising can drive brand share but share of voice needs to be higher than share of market, assuming of course that the product actually delivers, and a reasonable creative quality. Research also indicates that it is easier for a big brand to maintain and protect its brand share than a smaller brand. If a brand holds a share of 40% of a

# Example

In 1993 Safeway had a UK retail market share of 7.6%, trailing Sainsbury's at 11.5% and Tesco at 11.4%. Safeway had high margins but lower sales per square foot and smaller average shopping trolley than the two larger competitors. One reason for lower sales was that Safeway had failed to attract the big shoppers, families with children, who favoured Tesco and Sainsbury's. Even if couples did shop at Safeway they would tend to change to the other two once they had children. To attract families with children became one of several business and marketing objectives and the main communication objective. This obviously had to be done without alienating the existing customers.

The Safeway proposition was defined as 'Lightening the load' and a new spokesman was created, called Harry. Harry was a 3-year-old boy with a lot of charm, speaking with the voice of a well-known comedian, and taking the child's perspective on shopping in a humorous and very light-hearted way.

After five months Safeway's advertising awareness was 50% higher than the main competitors' and Harry was the nation's favourite, the second most popular advertising personality after the Andrex puppies. So many contacted Safeway that the company developed a special Harry video-show reel which consumers writing in received. The ultimate in advertising appeal, consumers sitting at home watching a video with commercials. Importantly, the advertising campaign was coupled with product improvements, i.e. changes to the store lay-out, range reviews and the addition of service facilities.

From 1993 to 1995 the average sales per square foot moved from £10.71 to £12.00. At the same time Sainsbury's sales per square foot hardly changed at all while that of Tesco increased as well, also due to excellent brand building activities (see relationship marketing).

A couple of years further on it appears that the campaign has lost some of its momentum. Harry was after a couple of years replaced by Molly who in 1998 got a baby brother and Safeway is no longer showing the same progress. Perhaps due to stiffer competition or Safeway suffering from being in a position of number three or four in the market place.

The Safeway example illustrates how an advertising campaign can go straight to a nation's heart by excellent and creative execution of a basically fairly traditional idea, shopping at Safeway is a good idea for a young family.

market, around 30–35% share of voice will be sufficient to maintain status quo.

What is good advertising? Many books and articles have been written on this subject but put simply, good advertising is advertising that builds brands and consequently generates sales. If sales go up when an advertisement is running, it is good advertising. The statement is particular relevant as experience as well as detailed studies indicate that a successful advertisement should generate sales from day one. Long-term effects rarely take place without short-term ones, an important statement as short-term effects are much easier to measure.

This simple rule is useful in retrospect but not when evaluating advertising. Professor Jones offer some additional advice on the basis of observing advertisements proven to be successful. These campaigns (all television commercials) are characterized by managing to hold the viewers' attention by giving them a reward for watching. This is done by making them relevant, engaging, entertaining, light-hearted and amusing, and doing so in a way that respects the public's intelligence. They are also often understated and visual. Professor Jones' research supports the battle-cry of many experienced marketers which is to ensure that 'the product is the hero' but done so that the functional benefits broaden into emotional values. Almost all successful advertising has the product or service as an integral part of the communication, explicit or implicit. No matter the product sector, whether perfume and other luxury items like Rolex watches, banking, cars or heavy construction engineering, cost-effective communication treats the product as the key communication element.

In short, commercials that are likeable and tell you something relevant in a way which is appealing rationally as well as emotionally, will most probably work. These conclusions have been reached on the basis of consumer marketing and traditional television advertising. There is no reason to believe that non-consumer advertising is any different.

Everyone recognizes the importance of creativity in developing good advertising but almost as important is consistency in core message, personality and even tone of voice. Many successful campaigns have been running for years, some in a virtually identical format such as the Andrex puppies, Rolex and Marlboro, others with some modifications, such as Coca-Cola and Levi's.

# Example

Andersen Consulting has during the 1990s advertised its consultancy services in a very consistent and appealing way, such as in the execution with a shoal of small fish turning itself into a large shark made up of all the small fish acting together. There are few products that are as intangible as consultancy but Andersen Consulting has been most successful in creating and developing a real brand in this sector. Awareness among business executives has grown from 15% to 90% and the consultancy is not only one of the largest but also one of the fastest growing.

Finally, advertising is often reviewed in isolation but it is a part of the marketing mix and the synergy effect can be very important. The basic rule is that one should not advertise without promotional support; by using promotional techniques to bring extra emphasis to the product is very sensible as it means greater cost-effectiveness in respect of advertising, but also in respect of promotion as the two work much more effectively in tandem than in isolation.

# 10
## PR – public relations

Public relations cover a very wide range of activities, some handled by PR departments and PR agencies like relations with the press, others by other parts of the company such as relations with the local community. In the following the more general perspective will be taken.

PR can be divided into pre-emptive activities, re-active and pro-active. They are all important for brand management but require different perspectives. The commonality is that in the main PR is focused on building the abstract values of the brand, in particular trust and confidence, although it is not exclusively so.

Pre-emptive PR, often grouped under the expression crisis management, should be part of all companies' marketing mix. What to do if the company, its brands or its facilities come under attack in one way or another. Mishandled crisis can be to great detriment for a brand, a crisis well-managed can sometimes boost key brand values.

## *Example*

The first one is PanAm and the so-called Lockerbie disaster. The chain of events was, in brief, that a bomb was smuggled on board a PanAm flight from Frankfurt to New York via London. The bomb exploded over the Scottish town of Lockerbie, a major catastrophe. PanAm, rightly or wrongly, got criticized for its handling of the situation and in particular the contacts with relatives to the victims on board but also the people of Lockerbie. The trust in PanAm was severely damaged.

*Example*

The second example is British Midland and its CEO Sir Michael Bishop. A British Midland aircraft, again very unfortunately, crashed outside Manchester on its way to land at the airport. As soon as possible the British Midland CEO went to the scene, talked to people, was interviewed live on television and generally showed concern and willingness to help. Somewhat surprisingly, it was later reported, that the confidence in British Midland did not, as expected go down, but it went up after the accident due to the way the crisis had been handled.

These two examples from the air travel industry can in short illustrate this, both related to unfortunate circumstances.

Technology is making crisis management more of a challenge as information can be disseminated much quicker, for instance via the Web.

*Example*

McDonald's was the subject of a long-running libel case in the UK, started by McDonald's to clear its name against various allegations. The opponent set out its argument on a website and within 24 hours it was accessed 35,386 times and the leaflet, which McDonald's challenged in court, was made available on the Web and, according to the press, 2.5 million copies have been printed off the site since 1990.

Another similar example is the problem of Intel and the initial Pentium chip where individuals used the Internet to publish information regarding the 'faulty' chip. A minor problem with the Pentium chip did in the end cause Intel huge amounts in recalling product and lost business.

Crisis management is not about building values, it is to protect and be prepared. The purpose here is only to draw attention to the problem, illustrate that it can happen to all kinds of companies and if the company is not prepared it can easily damage business and brand values.

Re-active PR is among the least exciting parts of the marketing mix, responding to requests from all kinds of people and companies. From a brand building point of view there is usually little potential in these kinds of opportunities as *ad hoc* activities rarely represents a perfect fit with the communication objectives of the brand.

The best advice is to refuse all requests in a very polite way, if necessary making references to similar activities the brand and company is supporting. Otherwise much time is wasted and proper brand management might suffer. (This does not include requests for information which should be responded to if appropriate.) This assumes of course that the brand values do not visibly feature openness or service in one way or another. It is also important to ensure that any promise in communication is responded to in the spirit of the brand. If you ask for comments, the comments have to be taken care of, answered and, if appropriate, acted upon.

Both crisis management and re-active PR are often more a question of limiting damage than pro-actively building values. Pro-active PR is more positive, a properly planned and executed PR programme can be very cost-effective in building brand values. It is an activity closely related to the next chapter, word-of-mouth, as the objective with many PR activities is to make people talk in a positive way about the brand.

PR at its basic is to establish relations with the media so that the brand is featured in a positive way. This can be achieved in any way from the classical press release to hospitality, showing the company, inviting people to sample the brand in whatever form, inviting journalists and others to meet key executives, and so on. This might sound trivial and old-fashioned but in many markets it can provide excellent results, assuming the basics are in place, with limited expenditure. PR can also involve sponsorship of events like dog food manufacturers sponsoring dog shows, or a bank sponsoring a rock concert to build the brand's position among the youth, their future customers.

Effective PR involves not only good preparation and execution but also a thorough understanding of what is relevant to the target group. The establishment of actors in commercials as stars in their own right, and the commercials as media event, has led to the opportunity to build the brand values of the commercial also in non-paid media. When a new episode of the Nescafé Gold

Blend story is to be screened, this is news for the press. Harry in the Safeway commercial (previous chapter) was the star not only of the commercial but also several magazine articles.

This phenomenon of the commercials achieving news value has been further exploited by linking PR and advertising.

---

## *Example*

When Harry's successor Molly was to be introduced in the commercials, Safeway ran a teaser advertisement in the television programme section of the newspapers stating 'When Harry met Molly . . .' and the time when the new commercial would be on air or 'Word on the street is that Harry is in love . . .' and a suggestion to watch the popular Coronation Street programme's commercial break (when the new Safeway commercial was screened).

---

Finally for many smaller brands, PR can be an excellent way of getting established. Red Bull, the energy drink, was almost exclusively established in London through on-the-ground PR, basically by going from bar to bar asking for the drink to create interest and then follow up with sales and activities. Total budget for the whole launch according to reports was £50,000.

Cars, especially luxury cars, often have a strong element of PR in the marketing mix, as have wines, spirits and cigars, categories where traditional advertising can be restricted as well as unsuitable from a targeting point of view.

PR can be very useful for building a brand. It has one distinct advantage over traditional mass media and that is that it is as appropriate for the small brand as the big one. In reality the small brand can be much more successful as it might get the sympathy vote as being the underdog.

# 11
## Word-of-mouth

One of the most exciting and most underrated parts of the marketing mix is word-of-mouth, that is activities and impulses by brand management to make people talk about the brand. In the old days, before advertising was established, it was the main communication medium for a craftsman to establish himself (or occasionally herself).

Word-of-mouth is a phenomenon which will take place regardless of the brand management plans to do so or not. The difference between spontaneous and incited word-of-mouth is that the chances are that the latter will be more useful in building the brand and that brand management is aware and can take action to push the talk in a specific direction. Word-of-mouth is sometime included under the PR heading but in the author's view it is a distinct activity and should be regarded as such. PR can pick up on word-of-mouth, can inspire word-of-mouth just as advertising but the management of it is a craft in itself.

Word-of-mouth is no doubt the most difficult part of the marketing mix to manage. The first reason is that the outcome is most uncertain, by doing or saying something a word-of-mouth chain of events can be started but whether it will work and spread as intended or in a different way is difficult to tell until afterwards. The second reason is that it can back-fire, just as some PR activities. If people through talking about a brand build a positive perception of the brand as for instance honest and ethical, and a representative then is suspected of wrongdoing the effects can be much worse than if no word-of-mouth had taken place. A third aspect is that the target can choose to ignore you and there is little you can do about it.

On the plus side, it is most probably the most cost-effective brand building communication method there is. You do not pay for media, as the target groups are the media and you usually pay nothing or very little for execution.

Restaurants and local traders live very much off word-of-mouth, as do many other suppliers. By providing extraordinary service or food happenings a local restaurant can get talked about and build brand values.

---

## *Example*

Hard Rock Café, especially in its establishing phase, is, or was, one of the masters of word-of-mouth. The restaurant chain, as far as I know, never advertises but is never-the-less one of the most well-known restaurant brands in the world. Whether people have visited or not, they certainly are aware of Hard Rock Café. Ways to get word-of-mouth going include the decoration of the restaurants with rock memorabilia; participation in auctions of such items, starting and finishing parties for rock tours; and not least the old night club trick of ensuring that there is as often as possible a queue to get in. After all, a place where people queue must be good.

The second string of the Hard Rock Café strategy is active merchandising, sometimes copies but often the real thing. It has been reported that Hard Rock Café earns half its revenues from merchandise. It makes a lot of sense to have people paying to advertise your brand, instead of, as most brands have to, pay to advertise.

---

Word-of-mouth is as a rule free but for the launch of Tamagotchi, the 'virtual pet' developed by the toy company Bandai, Japanese teenagers were recruited to talk about the product for a fee. Obviously with some success as the concept rapidly spread across both Japan and the rest of the world. The paid teenagers only had to start the process, it then took on a life of its own, as the idea obviously had great appeal.

Word-of-mouth is often combined with other events, advertising or PR. An extraordinary commercial can have benefits way outside of the traditional of creating awareness and building preference. If people talk about it for weeks after, the cost can be well worth it. The classic Rolls-Royce advertisement mentioned in Chapter 9 generated a lot of talk, extending the value of it way beyond the original placing.

Many companies run word-of-mouth campaigns without really knowing it; it is by accident rather than as part of a determined effort. It is much more likely that the talk will be beneficial for the brand if the right kind of stories are fed, if appropriate events are set in motion and that especially key executives act in the spirit of the brand values. Creativity in combination with always keeping the key brand values in mind is the key to successful word-of-mouth brand building.

What is commonly known as ethical companies, or companies with a social conscience, have a head start in word-of-mouth marketing as by definition they have a message which is by most seen as sympathetic, the individuals in charge are often nice people and people with a conviction, all factors which aid the process. Passion is important in all aspects of brand building but for word-of-mouth it is crucial.

## *Example*

Ben and Jerry of Ben & Jerry's Vermont Ice Cream are excellent representatives of word-of-mouth brand building. You just have to see them to understand that these two individuals love ice cream, are no ordinary business executives and they certainly seem like trustworthy guys. The Ben & Jerry story is interesting, relevant but far too long to be retold here so only a few extracts.

Ben & Jerry's was founded in 1970 in Vermont and in 1997 reached a turnover of $110 million. In one sense the marketing approach is very advanced, it is a totally integrated package and it is all based on Ben & Jerry, 'two regular guys living in Vermont, the land of cows and green fields, making some world class ice cream in some pretty unusual flavours' plus a sense of community responsibility, giving back something to the community.

Typical of Ben & Jerry's word-of-mouth building activities is the 'free cone day'. When Ben & Jerry started they promised that if they were in business the same day next year they would give all a free ice cream cone. And apparently they still do it and it is the kind of thing people talk about – and appreciate – especially as they also lay on free entertainment.

Successful word-of-mouth marketing requires enthusiasm and genuine involvement in the brand to generate the kind of buzz that will set off the right kind of word-of-mouth. And, as illustrated by Ben & Jerry, a sense of humour certainly helps. As many activities are short lived, as most word-of-mouth projects essentially are news and news gets old very fast, to rely on word-of-mouth for a main part of the brand building requires an almost constant stream of ideas and projects.

To illustrate from Ben & Jerry's:

- 'What's the dough boy afraid of?' campaign to stop Pillsbury, then owner of Häagen-Dazs, requesting that Ben & Jerry distributors who stock Häagen-Dazs should not stock Ben & Jerry's.
- Using social criteria when selecting suppliers, such as brownies for chocolate fudge brownie ice cream from a inner-city bakery in New York run by a religious institution to help homeless and unemployed.
- Merry Mulching event after Christmas when people can bring their Christmas trees and get them chipped up into mulch.
- A travelling circus bus providing free vaudeville shows all over the US.
- Free music festivals with Ice Cream Action – visitors can get a postcard and write to their representative in Congress about some issue and as a reward get a free ice cream.
- Factory visits. The Ben & Jerry plant is the main tourist attraction in Vermont.

The fact that Ben & Jerry's donate 7.5% of profits to a charitable foundation does of course not make the word-of-mouth less effective and it certainly illustrates that to be effective with this kind of brand platform you have to be honest and sincere.

While word-of-mouth is mostly applied by companies with strong and charismatic leadership such as Ben & Jerry's, but also Body Shop (Anita Roderick) and Virgin group (Richard Branson), it is not exclusively so.

All the examples mentioned refer to consumer goods but word-of-mouth can be as effective in business-to-business situations, although the approach often has to take a different slant. Scientific progress, extraordinary service or an element of eccentric behaviour can be ways of getting customer to talk in a positive way.

## *Example*

When IKEA opens, or re-opens after refurbishing, a new home furnishing store, the opening day is designed to create such attention
and interest, for instance by 'unbelievable' opening offers so that
people will talk about it for a very long time. When IKEA opened its
first unit in the New York area, there was a six-mile tail-back on the
highway, 26,000 visitors and the shop took in over $1 million on the
first day.

Also during the year local IKEA store management will create
events with distinct word-of-mouth appeal such as Swedish Lucia cel-
ebrations before Christmas or bringing in jugglers and clowns for a
special open day.

Word-of-mouth is an exciting, challenging and fun way of
building brands. It requires a lot of energy and creativity to do it
properly but any company, small or large, can have an element
of this in the marketing mix. It will be both enjoyable and cost-
effective.

# 12
## Direct marketing

Direct marketing is second only to personal selling as a direct and targeted communication. Properly executed it provides selected customers with relevant information.

The principles of direct marketing in building brands are very similar to other types of communication, the difference lies in the method and the potential for follow up. The methodology will allow customization, such as specific executions down to personalized greetings and contents, and split runs with follow up in the form of results and market research to see what will, or not, work. For details, see one of the many books and magazine articles which exist on how to best carry out direct marketing as most ideas have been tested at some stage.

Direct marketing is for many companies the life blood of the organization and it certainly is a most useful part of the marketing mix also for the business-to-business sector. It has been reported that one campaign for the *Wall Street Journal* has been running for 23 years pulling in some $1.3 billion.

The growth in direct marketing, quantity as well as quality, is to a significant degree an effect of computing power in that it has become increasingly feasible to run sophisticated customer bases and communication programmes.

While direct marketing is the tool to contact customers, relationship marketing is the term given to the marketing philosophy of building a closer relationship between supplier and customer.

Relationship marketing as such is nothing new. The sequence of listen, collect information, understand, communicate, sell, evaluate has been part of marketing for a very long time; but the difference is that with more computing power being readily available, the collection of data and subsequent analysis can now be mechanized. Decisions can be made based on hard data rather than the informed analytical guesswork of the past, the old tradesman technique is brought into the twentieth century. During the latter part of the 1990s it has become the fastest growing part of the marketing mix and an area where we have seen distinct advances in both planning and execution. With that follows the risk that this chapter will soon be outdated, if so, please accept our apologies.

The term relationship marketing can be interpreted in many ways but properly done should involve both a thorough understanding by the sender of the customer, an ability to customize the message and ideally also the product/service and the opportunity by the customers to communicate with and influence the company. Relationship marketing is relevant to all types of businesses. What is necessary to build a proper programme is a data base with customer information and transaction data, i.e. purchases and/or usage of products and services.

The starting point is the customer data base which will allow customer segmentation based on available internal factual information and the understanding that not all customers are equal, some are more important than others. On the basis of segmentation the brand can develop a direct marketing programme which will be customized to the customer base and then measure the response. Because the programme captures transaction information it is not necessary to use direct marketing, any communication can be used even normal advertising, but the tendency seems to be to use direct communication as it is when properly targeted usually cost-effective.

The results of the campaign are recorded and can influence the next planning cycle (see Figure 12.1).

The Tesco case in the example requires three additional comments. One is that the cost of the reward scheme, direct mail programme, etc. was balanced by a decrease in traditional televi-

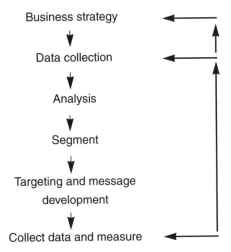

**Figure 12.1**   *The relationship marketing process
(source: DunnHumby Associates)*

# Example

One of the most successful relationship marketing programmes in Europe is the Tesco clubcard. The Tesco clubcard is from the outside no different to traditional loyalty schemes operated by petrol stations or most airlines with frequent flyer schemes. The difference lies in the application of the data.

Tesco, for many years the number two retailer in the UK, overtook the previous brand leader Sainsbury's in 1995 and by 1996 was almost two percentage points ahead of the rival. It has been claimed that a driving force behind the growth has been the relationship marketing programme symbolized by the Tesco clubcard.

The clubcard is a simple plastic card, not a credit card, identifying the customer so that his/her purchases can be individually recorded in the central data base. The consumer benefit is that on the basis of purchases, the customer is rewarded with money-off vouchers, fixed amounts in relation to money spent. In addition the customers get promotional offer coupons. On the face of it a 'loyalty' card programme, paying customers to stay loyal. The card is very popular, over 14 million issued in a country with about 23 million households.

The loyalty effect is important in itself. Published market research indicate that in 1996 Tesco gained 46% of its shoppers repertoire, ahead of all other retailers, and it is the scheme most used by the shoppers. Presumably well worth the reported £60 million Tesco paid out in one year to reward their customers.

The loyalty effect is however only part of the story. Additional real benefits are both information to fully understand customer behaviour and to use the information to develop, promote and build all elements of the Tesco brand marketing mix in a more cost-effective way.

By analysing customer purchasing patterns, evaluating response to promotions and using this information in the building of the brand, Tesco has achieved something quite unusual, getting to the Number 1 spot through organic growth after being number two for decades.

The effects can be very direct and simple. The card made it possible to ensure that an 80-year-old lady would not get a discount voucher for twelve cans of Coke but for a pack of biscuits instead.

sion advertising so the net cost was probably fairly small. The second point is that the scheme has been copied now by all the leading retailers. As in the Tetley round tea bag product development case it appears that the imitators gained very little. This is probably due to two factors, one is the 'being first' effect in itself, the other is that to run a proper relationship marketing programme requires skill and know-how, something that will only come with time. Industry observers state that it takes at least three years to get the benefits so if you are first in your market sector you will also have a learning curve advantage. The third point is that the relationship marketing programme was by no means the only factor behind the Tesco success. Keener pricing and better service have certainly also been of importance.

One warning, though. The loyalty achieved by a reward scheme is not brand loyalty in the true sense of the word. If the purchasing loyalty is an effect only of the rewards, once the rewards stop, the loyalty will change. It is only if the total programme will build a stronger brand, the result will be long-term customer loyalty.

Relationship marketing is an interesting opportunity to both better understand and more effectively communicate with the customer base. The main requirement is access to both transaction and non-transaction customer data. Another requirement is the amount of data. Grocery retailing is ideal given the amount of transactions by the very nature of the business, banking is another such business.

For a classic FMCG brand the situation is different in that pure transaction data are usually not available and frequency of purchase and the amount spent on each occasion is low. Pure transaction data are, however, not the only way to collect customer data. Promotions, coupons, competitions and other ways of communicating with the consumers can provide the raw material for a customer data base. Heinz UK have a direct marketing programme built around a consumer magazine with various offers, which has made it possible for the company to get into a dialogue with the consumers.

Business-to-business suppliers have in many cases a long tradition of direct marketing, writing to customers with relevant information. The customer base is often well-known and identified, the addresses are on file anyway for invoicing, etc. and other media are often not cost-effective or even available. The business-to-business sector offers plenty of opportunities to apply relationship marketing as the supplier often has access to transaction data as well as other types of customer information. An obvious example is a supplier of consumables such as office stationery but also more traditional businesses can benefit.

For business marketing one has to pay special attention to the customers' purchasing process. Who is the decision maker, or, perhaps more accurately, who is the real and who is the formal decision maker? Are these individuals identifiable with the help of invoice and payment data, or will it take other methods to get the information?

Direct marketing, in particular in the context of relationship marketing, is a tool that all brand builders should consider as part of the marketing mix. It is not appropriate to all businesses nor indeed to all brands but given the potential all should consider it. It is also my view that it is not advisable to rely totally on invisible means of communication such as direct marketing. Extrovert communication like display advertising has the benefit of giving additional social acceptability and credibility to a brand which in most instances is important, although not crucially so. If, like a retailer, the brand is visible anyway, this is not very important but for other market sectors such as financial services, it can well be a relevant consideration.

Direct marketing can make it possible to build brands cost-effectively. A relationship marketing programme can open up interesting opportunities to establish a link with the customers; communicate, understand and promote. While it is not appropriate to all brands, the tool set should be closely followed by everyone.

# 13
## Design

Design as a marketing mix discipline is often connected only to FMCG and the design of packaging. Design is however a much wider concept. For a retailer it includes the design of the outlet, exterior and interior, and also many industrial products are designed, or could be. It is only the totally invisible services which do not allow any formal design. The importance of design is apparent when considering that a poor design costs as much to execute as a good one, attractive design can have a major impact with the customers and that in most instances the cost of a good design is minute in relation to the positive effects.

This is most easily put into perspective in the classical design territory, FMCG. The outer of the product, what people look at and evaluate at the point of purchase is without doubt the most important part of the communication mix for these brands. It is important as it communicates at the point of purchase, thus the most crucial moment in the purchasing process, it is at work for the brand for 24 hours a day, 365 days per year and it is for many brands the only communication channel. In addition it often has secondary effects when the consumers are using the product at home. A tremendous amount of communication, 'opportunities to see', is often suboptimized or even mishandled.

How to brief and create pack design is no different from other types of communication but it is a craft that requires specialist skills as the physical as well as legal aspects do set limitations on what is possible. The role is to communicate the brand profile, the facts and the emotions, and to do this in a way that creates attraction for new customers and builds value and assists in creating over-satisfaction to ensure repeat purchases with the additional challenge that it has to be functional.

In design development and in particular for consumer goods and services one has to recognize that the design is the fundamental recognition signal, in a way a larger version of the brand logo. In this respect it is important to recognize that the design of a product requires updating with some regularity in order not to look tired, but also that any change should not be too dramatic so that the customers will feel lost and cannot find the revamped brand. Gradual change with certain intervals is the recommended approach.

To evaluate whether a design is an improvement or not is often quite difficult but one observation is that if a new design when displayed alongside the previous one does not lead the customers to pick the new one instead of the old one, then something is wrong.

## *Examples*

The Absolut Vodka story started by a couple of enthusiastic executives in the Swedish state monopoly for the production of alcoholic drinks and led to Absolut becoming the largest imported vodka in the US. An important part of the brand appeal was the bottle, inspired by hand-made bottles used for vodka-type products in the eighteenth and nineteenth centuries. The cleanliness of printing the product name directly on the bottle was another part of the design consistent with the values of a pure vodka, as of course is the name Absolut, a play on Absolutely pure. The bottle and the name, the latter combined in advertising with other words such as Absolut Christmas, Absolut Evidence and the famous Absolut Warhol for an advertisement featuring the bottle painted by Andy Warhol, became key parts of building the brand.

Ferrero Rocher is another example where a striking design is achieved by turning the traditional one on its head while maintaining practicality and functionality. At a time and in a market where all boxed chocolates were packed in boxes with fancy print, Ferrero packed its product in a transparent box so that the golden wrapped chocolates inside the box were visible already on the shelf. The transparent box retains with the help of the golden wrappers the luxury character necessary in this market, it is easy to display and turn into different pack sizes, and it is different.

Design in the wider sense of the word is of course very effective in retailing and other services where it is important to attract the public. Body Shop and Gap are just two examples. The design is also important in the context of restaurants and bars; and one interesting example is the spread of Irish pubs around the world, from Reykjavik to Calcutta and even Shanghai in the People's Republic of China.

---

## *Example*

The creation of Irish pubs is, however, no accident, it is part of Guinness' strategy to build markets for Guinness stout. Even in Britain the effect of Irish ambience on the consumption is dramatic, from perhaps an average of 2 kegs a week to 40 in an Irish theme pub.

The Irish pubs are run by local entrepreneurs, or Irish ex-patriates, but Guinness provides advice and not least the contact to and support for a design company to build a genuine Irish pub. The pubs are built in Ireland, including Irish bric-a-brac, then flat packed and shipped to the destination for reassembling. A related company provides Irish bar and catering staff.

By providing an Irish environment, and as an Irish pub, especially abroad, 'cannot' be without Guinness, the Irish origins of the brand are not only exploited successfully, the market position is actually enhanced as the brand and the environment work hand in hand to reinforce the brand values.

---

The definition of design differs and whether brand communication such as catalogues, instructions and web sites is advertising, promotion or design is open to debate. What is important is that all communication channels are fully exploited to build the brand and at the very least is consistent with the brand personality.

This also applies to industrial design. Braun, in the consumer market, has made industrial design a key part of the brand personality and the opportunity to do the same thing in consumer goods as well as industrial ones is there. It is a very cost-effective way of building the brand and at the same time an identity, and it rarely costs more than the standard creation from the desk of an engineer.

# 14
## Distribution

Distribution is not always included in the marketing mix but it remains a crucial part of most products and services for the very simple reason that if you as a customer cannot get in touch with the product, you will not buy. The Coca-Cola objective from the start of World War II to put Coca-Cola within reach of every US soldier has proved to be a very effective builder of business. Coca-Cola remains one of the world's absolute masters of distributing its product, making it one of the world's biggest brands.

Many marketers ignore the importance of distribution. It is an activity often handled by a separate department far away from the marketing group or increasingly contracted out to specialist companies. This ignorance can be an expensive mistake. Coca-Cola illustrates that in order to totally control a brand, you also need to control the distribution, regardless of who physically moves the goods. While distribution used to be a simple activity of ensuring that a product was transported from the place of manufacture to the customer, it is now more complex involving other aspects and providing opportunities for building strong relations with customers.

Distribution is usually thought of in the context of products but of course also services must be distributed, first be put in front of the customer to get a sale and then, more challenging, when providing the service. With services it is not only the challenge of distributing it, i.e. for instance getting the staff to the right place at the right time but also to control the quality. How to do that is outside of the scope of this book other than to observe that it is a distinct management skill. Some companies are much better at this than others.

The advent of e-business via Internet or Extranets can well put renewed emphasis on the distribution dimension. While tangible products will continue to require physical distribution, for software, images and other media-related products the distribution pattern has already changed and similar changes will take place in other sectors. The 24-hour availability of banking and other financial services does not only change the distribution pattern but also customer expectations, 9–5 opening hours on the high street is not enough any more.

From a marketing perspective, distribution is one of the most powerful links for several different reasons, all based on the fact that the physical distribution is not all, with it goes activities such as order-taking, invoicing and stock management. This has implications both from the traditional distribution perspective and the future one.

In a future perhaps totally dominated by e-business the ownership of a brand can be put in jeopardy if the new environment is not managed in a proper way. With changes in how business is conducted, a risk is that the control of the customer relationship might disappear from the hands of the traditional brand owner to the new intermediary controlling the new customer interface, with an end result of the brand no longer being a brand and the company only one of many subcontractors. The best insurance is a strong brand and being alert to changes so that the distribution initiative is not lost.

In many markets distribution is a barrier to entry. It can cost quite a lot to set up a distribution system, such as supplying soft drinks to fast food chains. In some markets outside contractors are available to carry out the work, such as to serve supermarkets, but in other cases less so, for instance to supply beer to bars, cafés and restaurants. The link between brewers and pubs in Britain was felt to be so strong that the Government introduced legislation to break it up to foster competition.

The increasing use of partnership sourcing, i.e. building close links between supplier and customer to share data in order to decrease stock holdings and develop more suitable products and services, has meant that there is, for the customer, a barrier to exit. To break one relationship and set up another costs time and money, both often in short supply, which means that the existing supplier has an advantage. From a brand leader's point of view, supply partnerships are well worth encouraging as it can help to isolate a business relation from frequent competitive tendering.

Both the barrier to entry and exit do little to build the brand, they are business tools. Understanding and using the process to the brand's advantage is, of course, very important and the prudent brand management ensures that these organizational aspects are not taking the place of proper brand building as with all links, however strong, they might one day break but used as an opportunity to build service values.

Another benefit from closer co-operation between supplier–customer is that it often involves exchange of information helping to understand the customers. This can be very important in planning the future of the brand.

Companies can sometimes build very strong positions for their brands on the basis of distribution strengths. Retailers getting the best locations and, as mentioned above, brewers integrating vertically so that they have a guaranteed outlet for their beer. The most successful example is probably Microsoft, using an original distribution advantage by becoming the system for IBM's personal computers, to build a total dominance of the software market so that it is in many cases almost impossible (with the exception of AppleMac) to buy a personal computer without getting Microsoft products.

The sale of personal computers is in itself an interesting example of the power of distribution. In the infancy of the market it was quite difficult for an individual to buy a PC, you usually had to go to a specialist shop, often in spirit if not officially operating in a franchised way, specializing in certain brands as the shops were too small to stock a wider range. This was expensive and for many not very satisfactory. Then Dell and a few others came along and started selling on mail order. Michael Dell's creation was a great success making Dell the world's fifth largest personal computer company. The traditional distribution system was sidestepped and the market changed.

As the market grew the next phase arrived with the computer superstore, the hypermarkets for computers such as PC World in the UK. With the new type of retailing also came an opportunity for aggressive selling by brands such as Packard Bell, providing ready-to-use computers often with software packages of great perceived value.

The development of the PC sales system illustrates that distribution advantages are not enough on their own. For a brand to survive in the longer term it has to be underpinned by strong brand values. Distribution advantages if available can provide very useful opportunities for short- and medium-term gain. For long-term gain they are no substitute for strong brand values and the company that combines both factors, such as Coca-Cola, is a very powerful competitor.

# 15
## Generating revenues

A brand can be the strongest in the world but if the company does not generate any revenues it is all a waste of time. The revenues are a function of volume times the selling price of the product or service carrying the brand and, of course, the stronger the brand the better the price.

The main objective for brand management is to limit the interest of the customers in the actual price. In an ideal world the brand is so strong that the customers do not really care what the price is. This of course rarely happens and the manager who is in such a situation will have to decide whether to charge high prices and generate a lot of revenue in the short term before competitors come in, or the customers wake up, or to price in a reasonable way and enjoy a more long-term relationship.

The price is of course of fundamental importance to a company and the setting of prices is something that should not be taken lightly or done by routine. The price in itself is important but also in most markets the price level influences the sales volume, the higher the price, usually the lower the volume and vice versa.

Pricing is also important as it can influence the perceived value of a brand. Some luxury items would probably be less attractive if sold at a lower price. Experiments have been reported where a low priced and a high priced perfume have been selling side by side and the high priced one has sold much better than the low priced despite being equal in quality. Such effects are unusual but it is worth recognizing that for many there is a correlation between price and quality and if the price is too low, the customer might well question the quality. The solution, assuming that it is in the company's interest to maintain a low price, is to explain to the customers why or how it is possible to sell at a lower price, giving some assurance that it is not due to poor quality but perhaps cost-effectiveness or clever purchasing.

To set the correct price is not an easy task, it is influenced by many factors, some rational, some irrational. The main difficulty is that price perceptions are first not necessarily accurate as outlined in Part 2, Chapter 5, and second are non-linear in character. Non-linearity means that while a price increase of 2% might not give any negative sales effects at all, 4 % might reduce sales dramatically (see Figure 15.1). In reality only experience and if possible experiments can provide guidance.

**Figure 15.1**    *Price volume relation for a fictitious brand*

The simple rule for pricing is that the price should be what the market is prepared to pay. This is classical economic theory but often ignored to be replaced with systems based on cost of production or average margins. Proper pricing procedure is to first set the price at a level the market is likely to accept, given the strength of the brand, the quality of the offer and the competitive situation, and then afterwards assess whether this is sufficient for the profit targets of the corporation. If the process is done in the reverse opportunities to increase margins might well be missed.

Price perceptions are difficult to judge but some guidance can be taken from being aware of what might influence the customers' potential reactions. First, the customers will look at a price in view of what he/she paid the last time, whether the previous price was relevant or not. When the then Soviet leadership increased the price of bread in the early stages of perestroika from being extremely cheap to just cheap, still lower than the price of the flour going into the bread, people rioted on the streets of Moscow. On a more mundane level, for one retail frozen bakery product in the UK, the on-going price level was £1.99 and sales were reasonable. A decision was made to promote at £0.99 in order to boost sales. The price has never returned to £1.99 as at that price, people will not buy any more.

Not only the historic price is of importance but also, not surprisingly, the direct alternatives. This is more relevant the more alternatives there are in the market sector and is one of the main reasons for ensuring that the brand is so strong that either the offer is seen as superior to competition, over-satisfying the customers, or is seen as having no direct competition.

The third aspect to bear in mind is the general price level. If inflation is high, price increases are expected, if the country is experiencing deflation, price decreases are expected. Brands that break the norm will in the first case get an advantage and in the second a disadvantage.

All this seems very straightforward but in reality is often ignored, even among the best and biggest. A classical example is Philips Morris and Marlboro in the US.

The example illustrates that Philip Morris, one of the world's most sophisticated brand management companies failed to recognize the changes in the price perceptions, or chose to ignore them. The case also demonstrates the non-linearity in that Marlboro clearly did not suffer from any sales decline at the early stages of building the increasing price premium, but then once a certain level had been reached, the effects were quite dramatic.

Pricing of an existing product has to take into consideration the various competitive elements, as illustrated above. From the perspective of developing brands, it is also important to retain a consistency across the brand portfolio as the brand will otherwise represent different pricing policies in different areas which will confuse and might cause perceptions problems.

---

## *Example*

The case is much debated but holds a couple of important lessons. In short the background was that Marlboro during the 1980s increased its price over the rate of inflation and over the rate of competitive brands. While the relative price of Marlboro went up, the brand share of discount brands increased by some 30%. To begin with Marlboro volume did not suffer at all despite an increasing price premium, it actually reached a brand share high of 26% in 1989. In the early 1990s consumers started to react by leaving Marlboro and the brand share declined.

In 1992 the price of Marlboro was cut by up to 20%, the share price of Philip Morris fell sharply but before too long sales of Marlboro recovered. While the stock market interpreted the price cut as devaluing the power of the brand, the reality was that the price cut saved the brand from disappearing. In other words, the sensible development would have been for the share price to increase.

---

For a new brand with a new product, the pricing does not, of course, have to take into account the historic situation but must on the other hand be set with care in respect of the competitive brands. To stand a chance of success and be seen as interesting Figure 15.2 usually applies.

In most cases it is the third alternative which is relevant, higher value, same price. There are of course exceptions, particularly in relation to new technology such as the introduction of quartz watches or new computers where higher value is available at lower prices but these sectors are more exceptions than the rule.

Increasingly companies apply flexible pricing, i.e. a special price for each customer depending on circumstances. This happens not only in businesses traditionally selling on specific quotes such as construction, but also in FMCG by suppliers to retailers and for instance by suppliers of office stationery.

Many products are distributed through a chain of companies. In such a situation it is important not only to price correctly to the end-user but also to make sure that reasonable margins are generated at the various levels. If companies on one level in the chain generate a relatively high margin while others get only the bare minimum, suboptimization is the likely outcome.

| Perceived value | Price |
|---|---|
| Lower | Much lower |
| Similar | Lower |
| Higher | Similar |
| Much Higher | Higher |

**Figure 15.2**  *Price – perceived value relationships*

Range pricing requires special attention and opens up interesting possibilities for competitive pricing although consistency with brand values should of course be maintained. If the range covers different executions and quality standards there is an opportunity to have items at a very low price to attract interest in the category, and then within the range introduce higher prices to cater for different target groups. How to structure the pricing within the range, where to start and where to stop, depends very much on the product sector. For a retailer with a price-value platform you start low and then try to move the customers up different steps. If you are selling more of a luxury and aspirational brand you do not want to start too low as that would send out the wrong signal and be inconsistent with the brand.

Many car brands do this with great skill, for value brands they feature a very low priced model to get interest but offer also various 'extra equipment' models. Others put the focus on the expensive models but the main part of sales are at the lower price end, although it is low price only in the context of the brand, not in absolute terms. Some Ford brands are examples of the first and BMW the second strategy where the expensive models are often featured but more 3-series cars are sold than of all the other models put together.

If the company is marketing several different ranges within the same product category, it makes sense to have overlapping ranges from a price point of view. This is particularly relevant in single brand retailing or other situations where a brand is in a dominant position. The original General Motors' strategy devised by Alfred Sloan with Chevrolet, Oldsmobile, Buick, etc. was to have overlapping brands with each one covering a specific segment but covering the top part of the brand below and the lower part of the one above to ensure broad market coverage.

While the car companies perhaps were the first to systematize this pricing strategy, it can be used for most range brands. It is also often used in restaurants, both for meals and in particular for wine lists. They usually contains a good value cheap wine; a second cheapest wine with a good margin for all those who do not want to be embarrassed by choosing the cheapest; and a couple of very expensive ones, almost never sold, which are there to demonstrate that the restaurant understands wine.

When setting the different prices it is important to remember that in addition to a suitably set lower and higher price, the items in-between are properly spaced out. Unless products are priced at the same level to enable efficient merchandising, promotion or generating a better margin, there is little point in having several products at similar levels. By spacing out the price levels it is likely that the total margin generated will be higher.

A much debated issue on pricing is the relevance of key pricing points, such as £9.90 or £999.00. Judging from the retail trade, and they are usually right, the sensitive price points do exist, however irrational they are. More products will be sold at £9.90 than £10.00. The consequence is that it does not make sense to price at £10.50, it is either £9.90 or at least £10.90, anything in between represents either a customer turn-off or a missed opportunity for extra margin.

For a company to review its brand pricing with the last two aspects in mind, range pricing and pricing points, can make a lot of sense. If this is done with a full understanding of the brand's position, the competition and the market place, the extra revenue and/or sales will be well worth the effort.

To correctly price the products and services is difficult and requires much attention and detailed evaluations. For the success of the brand it can prove to be crucial as only the 'right' price will generate the optimal mix of margin and volume.

# 16
## Managing the brand

The management of the brand is an activity which is of fundamental importance to a company's survival and prosperity. In most companies the main part of the brand management is the responsibility of the marketing department, which of course makes sense as much brand management is marketing management. This is, though, not a reason for top management to abdicate all responsibilities to the marketers. With the brands goes the reputation of the company, and that should always be a top management concern.

Top management involvement differs of course from market sector to market sector. For a one product/one brand company the CEO is the chief salesman and marketing manager, for a company with hundreds of brands, the responsibility needs to be delegated and the CEO will only take an interest in the most important brands. As an example of full involvement, the CEO of l'Oreal, the French cosmetics company, is reported to personally vet all pictures used in advertising.

Another reasons for top management to be heavily involved in brand management is the importance of continuity. CEOs stay longer in the company (in the UK over eight years) than marketing directors (on average slightly over four years) and marketing managers (on average 2–3 years). To ensure consistency which is important to retain the confidence of the customers, the involvement of the CEOs is a good 'insurance'.

How a marketing department should be organized for best

developing the brand is a cause for on-going debate. There is most probably not one solution, each company has to find its own ways. Sometimes a strict brand management model is the best as in the classical and often copied P&G model with the brand manager virtually as managing director of the brand; in other instances a trade sector approach can be more effective with specialists dealing with each set of customers and with a matrix of brand 'police' and developers. In several FMCG companies, the consumer and trade marketing is split into separate departments in order to get the best out of the brands in view of the retailing structure.

The spirit of the organization is often more important than the organogram. As outlined earlier someone in the organization must be responsible for developing the brand and controlling the brand. In addition one or two must be responsible for spreading the brand 'gospel' within the company. All parts of an organization have a responsibility to guard, promote and build the brand. To do so, they must be made aware and understand the core of the brand position and why this is so. For the success of a brand, the internal marketing is sometimes as important as the traditional external marketing, in particular in service industries.

In this context it is worth noting that the brand has a role not only externally, but also internally. Knowing the brand and being proud of the brand can do a lot to build employee morale. The brand provides a focus point, something to tie the employees to the company. This is, of course, good for staff morale but becomes a virtuous circle in that the internal brand focus makes it possible to build the brand in a more cost-effective, consistent and cohesive way; this makes the brand stronger among the customers which in turn boosts internal morale.

Marketing is by many seen as a young person's game. Experience is often not given much value which is unfortunate as the reality in many cases is that the most successful brands are managed by executives with extensive experience, while brands that have varying fortunes have often been exposed to rapid management change. Most examples indicate that to correctly evaluate and focus a brand requires experience and to implement the marketing mix, especially in a large organization, there is nothing as useful as having someone doing it who knows the organization and executives in other departments.

For brand management to be experienced is also important in order to match the customers' knowledge as they have often been dealing with the brand for a very long time. For consumer goods, customers often stay with the brand for 50 years (from the age of 20 to 70), which is in sharp contrast to the 18 months an average brand manager spends in one position. In such a situation the brand manager is at an instant disadvantage as they know less about the brand than the customers.

For experience to be of use, it must be coupled by monitoring systems so that a constant learning process takes place. It is sensible to ensure that for each brand a set of key brand indicators is identified and followed. The monitoring systems need to be accurate and relevant but not too complex.

---

## *Example*

For one company we worked with, a set of ten criteria was established and followed on a monthly basis. As a main brand was under competitive attack, in addition to defining the criteria and critical levels, possible competitive activities were discussed and decided ahead of time so that if a critical level was reached, or more accurately 'fell below the critical level', an emergency budget allocation was released and actions to fight off competition were implemented. The result was that the competitor never really got a foothold in the market sector.

---

While experience is important, even crucial, this must not be at the expense of creativity and willingness to experiment, especially the latter as creativity can be 'purchased' from consultancies and agencies. A constant programme of experiments to evaluate new ways of building the brand is strongly recommended as otherwise stagnation can easily set in.

Good marketing involves being analytical and systematic but flair and creativity is as relevant, preferably with a willingness to be opportunistic and take chances to make a difference. Many brand building initiatives owe their implementation to the determination of key executives. The Irish Pub strategy of Guinness was the brainchild of one Guinness executive and

Tetley's round tea bag was developed by a team of three.

On and off there is a discussion on whether marketing is an art or a science. The question is somewhat academic in that good art involves a scientific element, just as scientific development requires creativity, usually the domain of art. For building a brand, and ensuring that it is strong, requires a combination of a systematic, scientific approach and art in the form of creativity, both in the analysis and in coming up with the actual ideas. In both instances, a good portion of commonsense and understanding of business realities will help to ensure a long-lived brand.

## SUMMARY OF PART 3

The marketing mix is the set of tools brand management has available to build a competitive brand. Prior to briefing out the various activities, it is essential that the brand foundation is well-developed and defined, if not done properly, cost-effective brand building will be impossible.

The most effective marketing mix differs, of course, depending on category, market and country, each situation is different. However, in all cases both the product enhancement, whether OPD or NPD, and the communication need to be taken into account.

Two important aspects of marketing mix management are first to understand the on-going 'rules of the game' in order to adapt or 'break the rules'. Second, to continuously, or at least at regular intervals, reassess all parts of the marketing mix and, of course, the brand perception so that the brand is not declining but growing in stature.

# Conclusions

A competitive brand is a successful brand. If your brand is stronger than the competition you will succeed. If your brand is more trusted and relied upon than the others, the customers will choose your brand ahead of the others.

A successful brand is, however, not enough. Some companies do not succeed despite excellent brands, such as Apple. The skills in building a competitive brand has to be matched by an ability to run a profitable business and fortunately that is the case in most situations.

A strong brand will make a company more money than a weak one and a company that understands the necessity for a competitive brand will most likely be more profitable. A report by Citibank and Interbrand concluded that the most strongly branded public companies in the UK have consistently outperformed the FT-SE 350 index over a fifteen-year period. The companies included British Airways, Cadbury-Schweppes and Unilever.

To build a strong, competitive brand the main points are:

- Provide a superior product and/or service.
- Build the values so that you are perceived as better than the competition.
- Focus and create a distinct profile for the brand(s).
- Apply flair and creativity as well as systematic analysis and implementation.
- Lead the market.

# Reading suggestions

The following is a selection of books which I hope you will find interesting and useful.

Aaker, D. A. (1996) *Building Strong Brands*. Free Press.

Davidson, H. (1997) *Even More Offensive Marketing*. Penguin Books.

Deschamps, J.-P. and Nayak, P. R. (1995) *Product Juggernauts*. Harvard Business School Press.

Goldsmith, W. and Clutterbuck, D. (1997) *The Winning Streak Mark II*. Orion Business.

Gross, D. (1996) *Forbes Greatest Business Stories of all time*. John Wiley & Sons.

Hopkins, C. C. (1966) *My Life in Advertising & Scientific Advertising*. NTC Business Books.

Jones, J. P. (1995) *When Ads Work*. Lexington Books.

Kay, J. (1993) *Foundations of Corporate Success*. Oxford University Press.

Kochan, N. In Interbrand (1996) *The World's Greatest Brands*. Macmillan Press.

Kotler, P. *Marketing Management*. Prentice Hall, various editions.

Lager, F. 'Chico' (1994). *Ben & Jerry's: The Inside Scoop*. Crown Publishers.

Love, J. F. (1986) *McDonald's Behind the Arches*. Bantam Books.

Nilson, T. H. *(1992) Value-added Marketing*. McGraw-Hill.

Nilson, T. H. (1995) *Chaos Marketing*. McGraw-Hill.

Ogilvy, D. (1963) *Confessions of an Advertising Man*. Ballantine Books.

Ogilvy, D. (1983) *Ogilvy on Advertising*. Crown Publishers.

Ries, A. and Trout, J. (1981) *Positioning: The Battle for your Mind*. Warner Books.

Ries, A. and Trout, J. (1989) *Bottom-up Marketing*. McGraw-Hill.

Samuelson, P. A. (1980) *Economics*. McGraw-Hill.

Simon, H. (1996) *Hidden Champions*. Harvard Business School Press.

Treacy, M. and Wiersema, F. (1995) *The Discipline of Market Leaders*. HarperCollins.

Trout, J. and Rivkin, S. (1996) *The New Positioning*. McGraw-Hill.

Upshaw, L. B. (1995) *Building Brand Identity*. John Wiley & Sons.

# Index

Note: Figures in **BOLD** type indicate a reference to an example panel.

Absolut Vodka 206
action rules 118
advantages of old product develop-
    ment 161
advertizing
    barrier to entry 184
    branding 67
    building market share 184, 186,
    product experience 69
    'the product is the hero' 186
After Eight 104, **177**
Alcon 89
ALDI 36
Algida 92
American Airlines 64
American Express 49–50 96
American Motors 94
Ampex 116
Andersen Consulting 187
Andrex 27, 150, 187
appealing brands 54
Apple Macintosh 21, 211
Ariel 93, 102, 137
Audi 52
Avis 51
Bandai 194
banks 33
Bell's 82
Ben and Jerry's Ice Cream 195–6
Benetton 110
Benson & Hedges 106

Bishop, Sir Michael 189
BMW 38, 52, 60, **63**, 79, 90, 122, 218
Body Shop 54, 67, 196, 207
Boeing 22
BP 50
brand
    becoming a name 53–54
    building 65, 67–2
    categories 87–8
    criteria 52
    development sequence 119–20
    experience 64–6
    expressions 93
    first 116
    importance of 7–8
    management 26, 28, 215, 221
    managers 25
    names 58–60
    origin of word 57
    personality 133
    product development 156–8
    'real' 52
    repertoire 139
    role of 8
    servant of 170
    symbol 5
brand and product proliferation 7
brand developer 120
brand guardian 120
branding
    don't tamper 117

branding (*continued*)
  internal effects 221
  losers 117
  management involvement 220
  slow process 116
  strong values 49–50
  visual profile 50
  without advertising 67
Branson, Richard 9, 27, 104
Braun 206
briefing 144–5
British Airways 22, 51, 60, 167, 225
British American Tobacco (BAT) 106
British Midland 190, 191
British Rail 33
BT 174
Buick 218
Buitoni 89
business-to-business brand building
  10–11
Cadbury 116, 152
Cadbury-Schweppes 225
Café de Colombia 97
Camel 48, 107
Campari 92
canning food 151
capabilities 37
category defining 127
Chevrolet 218
chilled foods 154
Chippendale, Thomas 58, 59
Chrysler 94
Cinzano 183
Citibank 225
Clinton, Bill 49
co-branding 96–97
Coca-Cola 51, 130
  distribution 209, 212
  naming 60
  'New' and 'Classic' learning
    points 163, 164
coffee marketing 111
Colombian Coffee Federation 97
commercial messages 7
communication
  concept 134

strategy 166
Compaq 95
competitive
  monitoring 36–7
  perceived advantage 48
concept development 134
conceptualizing the reputation 69
consistency 117
corporate brands 88
cost-effectiveness 10
crisis management 187–9
Crosse & Blackwell 94
customer
  retention 15
  understanding 38
customizing 136
Daewoo 52, 143
Daimler-Benz 38
Dali 68
Daz 184
Dell 20, 211
detergents 137
Diana, Princess of Wales 49
Diet Coke 92
differentiating brands 52
Direct Line 156
Disney 22, 128
distinct brand values 52
distributor's own label (DOB) 96
Dr Oetker 89
Eagle Star Direct 157
Eastman, George 60
e-business 210
economies of scale 8, 9, 22–3
Ehrenberg, Andrew 22, 140
Electrolux 95
Esso 60, **65**
Eurostar 156
Eurotunnel 156
Exxon 60, **65**
Fairy 90, 91
Farmer, Tom 66
Ferrari 20, 122
Ferrero Rocher **206**
fighting brands 98
financial benefits 9

Findus 112, 117, 128
first in the market 22, 23
first in the mind 22
Fisherman's Friend 132
Flora 60, 174
focus 127
Ford 116, 128, 152, 217
  Mondeo 90
  R&D 148
fragmentation 156
frozen food market shares 143
FT-index 225
Fuji 130
Gap 207
General Foods 23
General Motors 121, 218
  R&D 148
Gevalia 112
Gillette 150, 160
golden rules 115
Guinness 92, 207, 222
Häagen-Dazs 182, 183
hallmarking 58
Hard Rock Café 194
Head & Shoulders 122
Heineken 152
Heinz 22, 89, 160, 162–3
Henry, Steve 167
Hertz 51, 52
Holiday Inn 60
Hoover 54, 58, 178
horseradish sauce 85
house brand 89
Husqvarna 95
IBM 11, 21, 148, 211
ice cream cones 91–2
IKEA 39, 54, 96, 197
Intel 11, 21, 97
  Pentium 92, 190
Interbrand 225
International brand strategies
  adaptation 111
  dual 120–1
  opportunistic 112
  uniform 109–110
Jackson, Michael 5, 49

Jaffa 54
Jagger, Mick 49
Jaguar 51
John Player 106
Johnson, 'Magic' 49
Jones, John Philip 181, 186
JVC 116
*Kaizen* 15
Kamprad, Ingvar 36
Kay, John 37
Kellogg's 59, 89, 105–6
Kent 106
key brand indicators 221
key value items 85
KitKat 89, 144
Kiwi fruit 55
Kodak 60, 89, 130
Kotler, Philip 13
Kraft-Jacobs-Suchard 23, 112
Kraft 59
Kwik-Fit 66
Lagnese 92
Le Shuttle 156
Levi's 8, 184, 187
Levitt, Theodore 150–1, 152
life cycle of brands 152
Lord Leverhulme 59
Lotus 130
Lucky Strike 106
Lynx 90
MacLaurin, Sir Ian 38
Madonna 6
Maggi 59, 128
Magnum 92
Manchester United 105
Marathon 70
market
  analysis 35
  leadership 19, 150
  pricing 214–15
marketing
  ethics 32
  first phase 14
  second phase 14
  third phase 15
Marks & Spencer 21, 67, 96

Marlboro  21, 107, 110, 216
Mars  5, 23
  Mars Bar  91, 92
  rebranding  70
Martini  183
Maxwell, Robert  128
McDonald's  77, 89, 90, 162, 190
McKinsey  5
Medcalf, Gordon  115
Mercedes  48, 52
Microsoft  9, 11, 21, 148, 211
microwave oven  155
Mitsubishi  104
Mozart  6
Napoleon  151
NatWest Bank plc  32
NatWest Visa  96
Nescafé  **66**, 160
  Gold Blend  144, 178, 192
Nestlé  **89**, 104
  frozen foods  112, 143
  branding  128
niche brands  140
Nike  34, 184
non-linearity in pricing  214
Nutrasweet  97
Ogilvy, David  181
oil lamps  57
Oldsmobile  218
Omo  93
Opel  69
Orange drink  128
l'Oréal  95
organizing brand management  220
oversatisfy  64, 66
own label  96
Packard Bell  212
Pampers  60
PanAm  190
paté  129
PC World  212
Pepsi-Cola  48, 130, 164
  re-branding  50
Persil  93, 137
personal dialogue  38
Philip Morris  215

Picasso  6, 68
Pinnell, Raoul  33
Polaroid  153
Polo  54
positioning  130, 133
  excluding  132
  reposition competition  132
  retailers  132–3
PR
  pre-emptive  189
  proactive  191–2
  reactive  190–1
Presley, Elvis  6
price
  points  218
  perceived  84
  range  217–18
primary brands  93
private label  96
Process development  148
Procter & Gamble  59  118  143
  'every day low price'  176
product
  brands  90, 92
  development  153–4, 155–6
  differentiation  7
  group brands  90
  life cycle  150–1
professional buyers  11
promotions  174–6, 191–2
purchasing process  63
quality  117
R&D  148
range brands  90
Reagan, Ronald  49
rebranding  69
recognition  54
Red Bull  192
Reichmann, Paul  48
relationship marketing  200, 202
Rembrandt  6, 58
Renault  111
Ries, Al  130
Rolex  73, 186
Rolls-Royce  21, 182, 195
Rover  79, 122

Safeway 171, 185, 192
Sainsbury's 39, 96, 122
sales uplift 174
Scandinavian Airlines 38, 39
Sears 106
secondary brands 94
segmentation 136
    brand loyalty 137
    cost of 137
    objectives setting 28–9
    sense of purpose 9
signatures 58
Singapore Airlines 51, 75
situation brand loyalty 140
SKF 23
Skoda 7
Sloan, Alfred 121, 218
Snickers 70, 89
Sony Walkman 155
Soviet television sets 48
Spice Girls 49
store cards 40, 200
Stradivari, Antonio 58
Swatch 148
synergies 143
Tamagotchi 194
Tango **16**, 167, **177**
targeting 135
tertiary brands 94–5
Tesco 21, 39, 96, **201–2**
Tetley Tea 151, 160, 222
Thatcher, Margaret 49
3M 60
transaction data 40, 203
transistor 148

Trout, Jack 130
trust 7
Uncle Ben's Rice 77
Unilever 89, 112, 143, 225
US automobile industry 32
US rail operators 127–8
USP 133
Valencia 54
value-added marketing 31–2
value
    dimensions 73–4
    enhancement 74
    spectrum 79–82
values
    abstract intangible 78
    attraction 64
    cultural aspects 80
    general 75
    negative 81
    specific 76
    'stored' 49
    tangible 77
VHS 116 155
Virgin 9, 28, **104**, 196
virtuous circle 66
Volkswagen 32, 52, 95
Volvo 38, **111**, 122, 134
*Wall Street Journal* 199
Wall's 92
Wal-Mart 36
Wankel engine 154
women's magazine 53–4
Xerox 53–54
Yamaha 104
Zespri 55